Famous Aircraft Series

The
F-86 SABRE

by R.J. Childerhose
Scale drawings: Richard Groh
(A Len Morgan Book)

AERO
A division of TAB BOOKS Inc.
Blue Ridge Summit, PA 17214

To the boys from the Stable, the pilots of
Overseas Ferry Unit, RCAF, 1953-1957.

ACKNOWLEDGMENT

A number of individuals and organizations assisted in the prepa-
ration of this book. Our thanks to David Menard, Brian Baker,
Dino Cerutti, Miss Peggy Penney, Bill Daniels, North American Aviation, the Magazine and Book Branch of the Department of Defense, and the Canadian Department of National
Defense.

FIRST EDITION
FIRST TAB PRINTING

Printed and published in the United States of America by Aero, a division of
TAB BOOKS Inc.

Library of Congress Cataloging in Publication Data

Childerhose, R. J.
Famous aircraft, the F-86 Sabre.

1. Sabre (Jet fighter planes) I. Title.
UG1242.F5C43   1987   358.4'3   87-111439
ISBN 0-8306-8649-5 (pbk.)

Every pilot has two favorite airplanes. The one that he flew at one time in his career and the one that he'd like to have flown. About the first of these he can wax lyrical. About the second, he can be interested. Fighter pilots are — who will quarrel? — more lyrical than the rest.

Recall the light of fondness in the eye of the Old Fighter Pilot when he talks of his tour on P-38's, Corsairs, Mustangs or T-Bolts. Obsolete now, but in the particular day of each, the best and fastest that flew.

There is a special pride-of-arms in flying the best fighter. It is this pride that persists, long after the airplane itself has been retired to nostalgia.

Some fighters—by battle honors won or sheer beauty of design—live in memory longer. Every country has them. The FW-190, the Zero, the Spitfire. It depends too, on the period of your life when you flew it. We remember best that airplane which affected our emotions

the most. The one we think of when recalling "the best days" of our flying.

For this writer, that airplane happens to be the Sabre.

It was a winner. That is as contentious a statement as I wish to make. For what follows is not a compilation of statistics—production figures by type, speed records and battle honors won—but a sentimental account of one pilot's affair with an airplane.

One thing more. Tales told by Old Fighter Pilots are sagas. Treat them as such. Away with you nit-pickers and carpers. You alleged truth-seekers. If you wish to argue extended wings versus slats, point fives versus cannon, look elsewhere. Sagas are sagas.

So be it. The OFP, grizzled, bent from by-gone G-loadings, gazes into the fireplace remembering. His pole hand clasps the post-parandial beer while the forefinger—in remembered reflex— stays loose.

Sabre 2 of 410 (Fighter) Squadron, RCAF, on low pass at North Luffenham, England, 1952.
Black smoke trail was characteristic of GE J-47 that powered Sabre 2.

First Sight

The Sabre Mk 2 (F-86E) was introduced to the Royal Canadian Air Force in 1951, and to this ab initio fighter pilot early in '52. The first Sabres off the Canadair assembly line had gone to equip the first three (of 12 total) RCAF squadrons to proceed overseas as part of Canada's NATO commitment. For this reason the fighter OTU (Operational Training Unit) at Chatham, New Brunswick, continued training fighter pilots on the twin-boom de Havilland Vampire.

The throaty roar of the General Electric J-47 which powered the Sabre was far different from the demented shriek of the Goblin engine in the Vamp'. Thus it was,

when the first two Swords were flown to a pine-surrounded Chatham one spring evening, not only students but the instructors too, tumbled out of the officers mess bar to watch the beat up.

As beats ups go—in retrospect—it was probably modest. Above building level. It was the sight of the Sabres themselves that was exciting. Swept wings and high fins. They looked shark-like. We were at the corner of the hangar in time to see the final pass.

Two toy-like Sabres wheel over the black pine forest. Invisible now, head on. No sound. Black smoke trails, a characteristic. They hump it over the last of the pines

First production Sabre 2 from Canadair, Ltd. wearing 410 (Fighter) Squadron markings. Note fibreglass nose and small drop tanks. Handle behind pilot's head was for seat raising and lowering. Photo taken over Montreal Island late 1951 or early '52.

and flatten close to the ground. No noise. Two silver Swords slicing across the deep-green infield. Whispering now. Ghostly shreds and tatters fllicker behind the canopies. Shock waves.

As the first Sabre lifts to clear the hangars, the whisper becomes a moan of tortured air. WHUMP! It's gone. Second Sabre lifts, hesitates, then barrels in the traditional victory roll. Half-way round it stops. Nose dips, sickeningly. It disappears behind the buildings.

"He's dead!" someone shouts.

He reappears, sliding along the horizon after his number One. Spectators laugh, nervously. Sweaty palms are wiped in pockets out of sight. No one admits to fright. We're all fighter pilots, aren't we?

"How about that guy," someone says admiringly of the Sabre pilot.

"He didn't mean it," says someone else.

Discussion, while all eyes watch the tiny silhouette Sabres join up for the pitch and landing.

"He was having trouble getting it round."

"Maybe he was trying to climb inverted."

Over our craning heads they pitch. Whistling thunder. Dive brakes sprout from the sides. On the downwind leg, stem-like wheels appear. Noses high, intakes sucking wind and tentacle wheels feeling for the runway. Puffs of smoke and we didn't recognize a hot landing.

There were too many wheels monopolizing the swept-back newcomers there on the ramp for an immediate examination. But we got our look next morning in the hangar early. The Sabres were parked amid Vampires.

"Look at the size of them!"

Compared to the diminutive Vampires, the Sabres were giants. In awe we circled the huge beast. Everything about it seemed radical. The thin and swept-back wings. The hanging slats on the leading edge. The towering fin, the 'flying tail' (entire horizontal stabilizer

moved) and the six point-five machine guns arranged three along either side of the nose.

The hanging ammo door looked too frail to stand on so we clambered up on the wing and thence to the cockpit.

"Man!"

The array of dials, instruments, switches and consoles seemed too complicated for mere Man.

"Look at the stick."

The pistol-grip control column had a variety of little red buttons, a red trigger under the pilot's forefinger and a round trim switch under his thumb. The throttle was also adorned with switches: a sliding switch for speed brakes, a mike button and another mysteriously labelled 'radar lock'. (Or something.)

The ejection seat had red handles. The instrument panel was black. VHF, radio compass and IFF transponder were on the right, gunsight on top of the instrument panel. On the floor, in front of the stick, was an impressive and baffling armament panel with red covered switches, toggle switches, and a rheostat dial. On this, apparently, you dialed the surface wind when dive bombing.

It hardly seemed possible that I would ever be expected to master that cockpit full of complexity. Yet the day would come when I thought it the most comfortable and reasonable of all cockpits. Nothing out of place. Everything in its place. From tail pipe temp to oxygen flow.

As we left the hangar, we paused for a last look.

"That one is bent," said my companion.

And it was. The Sabre that had done the low level roll the evening before, was twisted. More Sabres were to be similarly wrenched and written-off before we learned not to roll them at low level and max speed.

Sabre 5 or 6 instrument panel modified by RCAF's Central Experimental & Proving Establishment, Ottawa, for special tests. Note non-standard UHF selector on top left corner; secondary G-meter lash-up in top right corner. Tin plate above G-meters is for mounting test equipment.

First Flight

The first, or check-out flight for a pilot on a new type of aircraft, is always a memorable occasion.

We can't recollect our first Sabre ride. Except that it was preceded by much reading of pilots Handling Notes, and a blindfold cockpit check. Sitting in the cockpit of a hangar queen with a handkerchief tied round our eyes groping for things while someone stood on the wing saying:

"Flaps, okay. Oxygen, okay. Canopy defrost. Okay." Pause: "You just flamed-out. Do a relight."

Fumble fumble while the strained brain regurgitates. Throttle off, airspeed 185 knots, unnecessary electrics off. What next? Oh yes.

"I descend below twenty thousand before attempting a relight."

"That's what it says. You'll probably have tried three relights before then. What next?"

"Uh," intelligently. Paw the cluster of switches in right hand corner. "Check engine master and generator switches 'on,' and battery switch to 'battery'."

Sabre 5 of RCAF Station Trenton, Ontario on a practice flight. Loop sequence flown just east of Trenton over Bay of Quinte. Photo by Barry Herron. Circa 1954.

Sabre 2 over St. John's, Quebec, circa 1952. Note leading edge slat partially extended as Sabre wallows to stay behind T-33 photo ship.

And so on to the successful relight of sick J-47.

"It didn't light," says the unseen mentor.

"Oh? Well." Reactivate brain. Then, parrot-like: "If engine fails to relight before the aircraft has descended to five thousand feet, prepare for forced landing or abandon the aircraft."

"All right. Let's see you."

Ejection procedure. Again like the parrots.

"Lean forward and pull the handle up to jettison the canopy . . ."

"Don't pull it!!"

"I wasn't. I was just indicating . . ."

"Well get your hand off it."

"I wasn't going to . . ."

"Leave it alone. Just tell me what you'd do."

People were always nervous about seat ejections in the hangar.

The morning of our check-out was sunny. I remember it now. Ottawa in May. Sunny. Big Silvery Sabre parked in lonely splendor on an empty ramp. Big brother flight commander walking out there with you. Moral support. He had a fantastic total of 48 hours on type himself. He offered encouragement.

"Don't bend it."

"I won't."

"Don't bring it back u/s." (unserviceable)

"I won't."

"It's the only one we got," he grumbled.

Our squadron was in process of formation, or reactivation, since it had been a bomber squadron during the war. Being an ex-bomber squadron was difficult to reconcile. However, on the morning of which we speak, our squadron had five pilots and four airplanes. Two Sabres and two Harvards. One of the Sabres was unserviceable.

Between the two of us—him on the wing leaning in— we got it started. The noise was considerable. He was mother-henning the post-start check. Shouting in our ear.

"Dive brakes!"

Flick the thumb switch on the throttle.

"Alternate hydraulics!"

We select the appropriate toggle, then work the ailerons and watch the pressure needle dip. Grand. Why doesn't he get down?

"Radios!"

VHF 'on', radio compass flip, IFF to stand-by. There seems nothing else to do but go. Flight commander peers anxiously at our dial shop, then at the pilot.

"You okay?"

"Sure."

"You sure?"

Nod emphatically.

"Sure I'm sure."

"Put on your hat. It'll help."

It did too. The nylon headset (we had no crash hats then) helped considerably for attached to it was oxygen mask, mike, and built-in ear phones. Friend flight commander jumps down and walks determinedly away. Ground crew chap fastens hanging ammo door step and walks also determinedly away. The tower talks to me.

"Roger, Mohawk 29, blah blah blah, runway thirty-two, yak yak yak, taxi."

Runway 32. He said a lot of other things but for a long while the embryo fighter pilot could only assimilate the important things.

Sabre 5 over RCAF Station Trenton, Ontario, home of the RCAF's Training Command headquarters.

Sabre 5 of RCAF Station Trenton, Ontario.

At the end of the long jet runway we stop, set parking brakes, and think. Oh yes. Hydraulics harness hood trim pitot fuel flap gyros switches oxygen. The pre-takeoff check. Laboriously we went through this ritual, selecting half-flap and leaving the canopy open 'til the very last.

CLUNK. Sealed in.

"Mohawk twenty-nine. You ready for take-off?"

What's wrong with him? It's my fuel isn't it? But we say 'yes' and he says 'go' and we're out on the big wide runway with a J-47 behind us winding up to screaming 5200 pounds thrust. Tail pipe temp stabilizes at upper green line. Green means go. That's as much as anyone should ask a fighter pilot to remember.

White strips down the middle. Flick flick flick and man that's fast. Eyeballs off the windscreen. Where's the airspeed? There it is. Funny little barber pole for Mach reference confuses things. 100 knots! Runway pouring under us. What speed? Nosewheel off at what? Lift off at what?

The Sabre went flying.

Next? Wheels wheels! Fumble for the little wheel in the left hand corner. Don't overspeed the gear. 150 knots on the dial. Whew. FLAPS! You forgot the flaps. Zonk. A fast left hand rams the flap lever up the quadrant. Why are you panting? And why are the wings rocking?

The Sabre is so sensitive on the ailerons that we are climbing all awobble. Remove the hand from the pole. There. She flies better without.

The only other impression of that first trip we recollect are those of speed and incredible lightness of control. The ailerons in particular. Out of sheer exuberance we flew for miles in slow and fast rolls. They were ridiculously easy. Too soon our forty-five minutes of airborne endurance was over and it was back to the airfield.

"Mohawk two-nine on the pitch."

Oops. Almost half-rolled. Uh! G drags at your arms, pulls your eyelids and weights your neck. Relax the stick pressure and the Sabre porpoises there a thousand feet over the field in plain sight of a thousand spectators. Or so it seems.

185 knots on the downwind, gear going down. Clunk thump clunk as unseen D-doors snap into position. Half-flap on base leg. Bend her round. Harder. Oops. Overshot on the final turn. Oh well, proceed like the snakes. Trim back, back some more. Speed falling. Rest of the flaps. Runway underneath. Back, back. Power pulled. Where's the runway?

Bump bump. Mainwheels on. Grand. Nose settles, gentle bump. Sabre rolling down the middle. A piece of cake, as they said in the bad old days of World War II.

Taxi in and shut her down—throttle round the horn. The insensate shriek of idling J-47 chokes and dies in ever-descending decibels. The breeze across the ramp feels good on a sweaty muzzle as we unfasten the rubber mask and let it swing. There are no friends to greet us.

"How is she?" asks a sergeant.

"Okay."

He walks away. Unfasten harness, oxgen, radio, plugs. Seat pins replaced. Okay? Man, she's a dream.

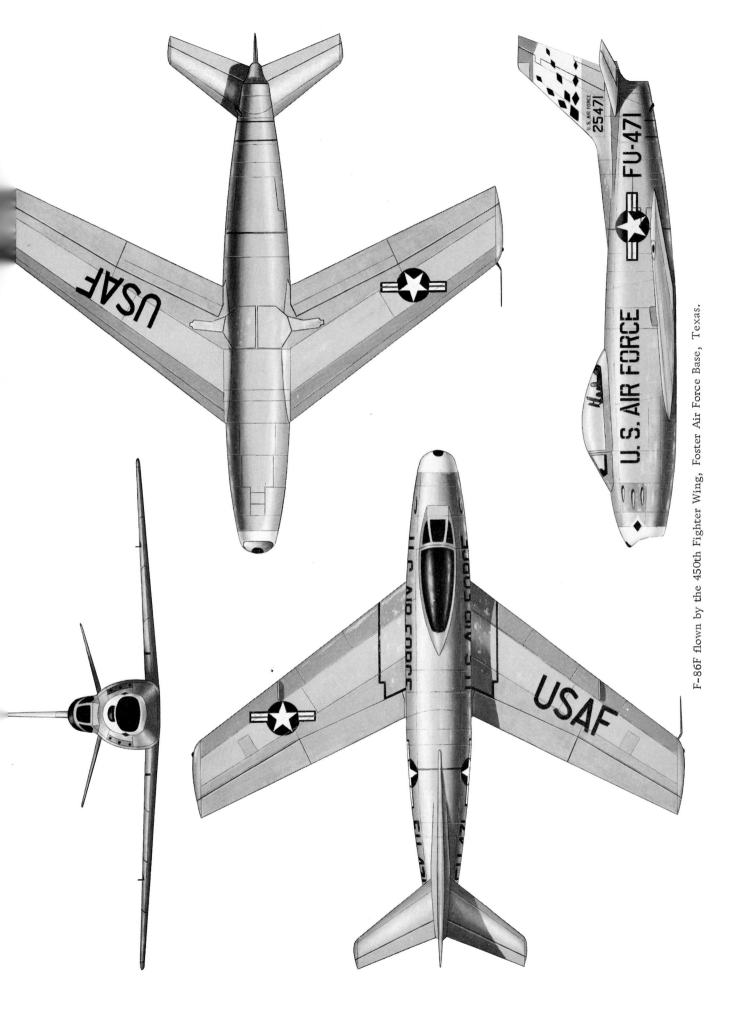

F-86F flown by the 450th Fighter Wing, Foster Air Force Base, Texas.

One Sabre Confirmed

Sabre conversion in these early days was something less than formal. I believe there were eight or ten familiarization flights scheduled, wherein the incipient fighter pilot was allowed to try the qualities of the Sabre by order of difficulty. That is, you tried acrobatics one day, height climb the next, Mach-run another day and so on. But naturally everyone did everything the first or second trip.

Return, friend reader, to the flight room. Said illustrious flight commander:

"We got three serviceable. We'll try some formation."

The briefing was brief, for the ethos of WW II fighter days was still upon us. This was soon to change, but we didn't know it then.

"Start up on channel two and listen out," concluded glorious leader. "We go."

On the start, our three-plane formation became a two-plane as my buddy Keith went u/s.

"Mohawk Red, taxi two," said flight commander's dulcet voice in our headset.

"Roger Red. You're cleared etc and etc," replied the tower. And since we were just a wingman, we didn't even have to listen for the runway number. There are certain advantages to being a follower of men.

Just as the pair of us got airborne, and the wheels began their hydraulic journey into the wells, Keith came back on the air.

"I'm serviceable. Wait for me."

So we orbitted under a broken layer layer of summer cumulus. Beautiful day. Columns of sunlight mottling the verdant countryside below. Not that citizen pilot here had time for sight-seeing. That first formation trip in a Sabre kept him busy racking the throttle from 'idle' to 100% trying to stay in position.

Keith joined up and leader pointed his silver Sabre at the first patch of blue that presented itself. Whaff. Through the cu' and into the blue above. Bright sunlight, dazzling cumulus spreading like a sea. The sea receded.

"Okay Red, echelon port."

Our time. Gently gently. Throttle back, ease her down and start the slide across. Eyes glued to the charcoal orifice of the leader's Sword. Sliding back. Whang! Power on. No result, for acceleration is all but nil.

Slowly and eventually we skid back into position, this time looking at the other side of leader.

He regards us. Contemptuously? He appears bored.

Eventually leader calls for a fuel check. Keith has 200 pounds more than me due to his belated start.

"Okay Red. We'll go home. Channel seven go."

Channel seven was 'homer' frequency.

"Steer two six zero," said the man.

There is something comforting about voices that tell you which direction to fly.

So we flew and flew until it seemed surely we must be getting close to Ottawa. Red leader decided to take us

down for a look. Down down toward the swelling white ocean of cloud we went. Most of the sweat was in keeping formation, although a sense of anxiety had now replaced the comfort instilled by the ADF operator. Baff. Through the cumulus and into the grey shade below.

Trees. Nothing but trees. Glorious leader is upset.

"Homer," he says, "check that blasted heading."

And he points us up like an aerobatic team to where fuel supplies are known to last a little longer. Into the bright blue above. Sunlight glinting on three scared Sabres.

"Oh." The small uncertain voice belongs to homer. "Try zero nine zero. I guess I gave you a reciprocal."

The leader's unannounced turn-about was so abrupt that his wingmen failed to hack it. Which was too bad. After blacking-out in the attempt to follow, we could do little but straighten out on the suggested heading and fly home. Alone.

We listened to Red leader discussing things with homer, and when he took himself to tower frequency, we switched too. After the yakking died down, Keith and I checked in. Both leader and tower seemed glad to hear from us.

"Roger, Red," said leader. "Return independently to base."

Fuel gauge in the right hand corner was pessimistic. What happened when it dropped to zilch? Pouf? Is a flame-out 'pouf'? And what happened after that, naturally, was: head forward raise the handle head back feet in the stirrups squeeze the trigger . . .

"What's your fuel state, Red Two?"

That's me. With a start we check the pointer.

"One hundred pounds."

"Okay. Continue. Red Three?"

Continue? The clod. What else could we do? Keith had 200 pounds more go-juice than me. It was enough to get him back to Ottawa.

Sunlight. Cloud below and a white hazy horizon stretching ahead. Fuel gauge continues functioning. Beautifully in fact. It reads 'zilch'.

"Ottawa tower, Red Two here. Gas gauge reading empty but I've still got a fire."

"Roger, Two. If you descend below cloud you'll probably see base."

It's a comfort to have people on the ground telling you what to do. Sprogs have been known to listen. Back with the throttle, down with the nose. Zap. Through the cumulus cloud once more.

Trees. Nothing but trees. Pouf went the J-47. 2300 feet said the altimeter. Down said the airspeed, down.

Too low to eject. Happy hum of engine dies, is replaced by the shriek of wind. Patient trees await the arrival of Progress.

"Red Two just flamed-out."

"Bale out! Bale out!" says somebody.

"Force-land on the nearest runway," says another.

"Try a relight," suggests someone else.

The cacophony of voices makes thinking difficult.

Snap with the VHF. There. All that yakking cost 500 feet. To the left and behind, three miles perhaps, six small hay fields in the shape of an L. Board fences separate the fields. But what are weathered boards compared to stout healthy trees?

Set up a pattern using the top end of the L for a threshold. Airspeed 185. Tum-te-dum-dum. Switches off. Harness cinched then locked. Ugh. Can't move. Wind noise outside. Canopy open? Why not? Navy pilots land with canopy open.

Along with the unexpected blast of cool air, comes the low unmuted shriek of the wind. Unsettling. Check check. Airspeed 185. Swing onto a crosswind leg. High? Speed brakes, to save the flaps. Might need them on the approach. 180 knots. Okay, let it come back. Gear up.

Looks fat. Airspeed, height, turn on approach. A row of trees blocks the near end of the selected field. Another row bisects the base of the L. Why didn't we see these before? Four fields from those big trees. Surely we wouldn't go that far.

Quick S-turn to hit the L at an angle, aiming toward the bottom arm of the L. Just in case. As for the near trees. Tum-te-dum-dum. We'll just nip over the top of them, dump the flaps and set her in there.

Trees at near end are small, perhaps 20 feet. Drop the nose. 150 knots. Good, good. Shoulder harness is tight. It's too tight. Wish I'd been more careful. Now isn't the time to mess with harness. Level with the tops of the trees now, the green foliage swells toward us. Flashes by in a green blur. Self-confidence retreats and we forget the flaps.

Level out over the sun-burned hayfield. It pours back under us. Endlessly. Check back, back. Ease back on the pole. Where is the ground? Swish! First fence hurtles beneath us. Three fields remaining. The giant elms wait patiently. Surely we won't go that far. But we boot rudder and point at a gap in the trees anyway.

Rumble rumble rumble. Tail dragging on the grass. That feels good. Ahead of us, obscured by uncut hay, is a rock pile. Not high. Three feet perhaps. But, yipe! Back on the pole. Sabre hauls herself up out of there. Stalls.

Ka-WHANG! Tail pipe catches the rocks and Sabre slams the ground. Bounces. Retrieving hands and head, we lock onto the controls. Where's the gap? Shove rudder and get some response.

KRUMP!

The smooth force-landing degenerates into a series of sickening crumps. The instrument panel is a blur and the air is filled with wood and pieces of aluminum. We're being thrown about the cockpit. Hang and rattle. If they find you dead let it be with your hands on the controls.

CRASH! Another fence, and again the sky is filled with wood. We're through the trees in a roar of rending metal. Sabre skids and skitters to a final halt.

Mechanically we go round the cockpit killing all the switches, uncoupling the oxygen and radio leads, releasing the seat harness. It feels good to unfasten the oxygen mask, to stand up in the cockpit, to step out onto the ground. A rich cascade of blood pours down when we peel the nylon headset from our skull.

No problem. We feel great. A cool breeze rattles the leaves of the elms and dries the sweat on our face. The Sabre is demolished.

What happened? The air force took the view that instead of a number Two following his leader to the point of fuel exhaustion, the number Two is captain of his own aircraft and responsible for its safety. It only hurt when the nails were going in.

Sabre 2 write-off, August 22, 1952. Author ran out of fuel 30 miles short of the runway. Force-landing near Carleton Place, Ontario. Log fences inflicted heavy damage; stump sheared port wing.

Diamond-four of Sabre 5's belonging to #1 (Fighter) Operational Training Unit, Chatham, New Brunswick. Large numbers on side are final three digits of serial number; were helpful in finding the bird in long line-up on the ramp. Note the slot-man using 15 degrees of flap. Some pilots liked it but danger lay in over-speeding them with resultant damage.

Bad WX Days

As summer faded into fall, the good weather days were more noticeable for their absence. The Sabre flying didn't change so appreciably, since our flight commanders persisted in the ethos of WW II: 'A ceiling, chaps. Get airborne.'

So we trundled out, in rain or murk, dank or snow.

"Mohawk Green is ready for take-off."

"Okay, Green. How many in your section?"

"Four. Didn't you get our flight plan?"

There was no flight plan.

"No. Are you at the button of three-two?"

"Affirmative."

"Okay. Green is cleared for take-off."

So we flew. None of us held instrument ratings. Perhaps this was a reason none of us thought too much about weather, or about getting back down if we once got up. With a radio compass, ADF homer and GCA, all there to help, where lay the sweat?

We lost a few, naturally.

The crux of the problem was the fact that we all insisted on behaving like fighter pilots. The spirit of the Tiger was upon us and it was irritating when outside agencies sought to impose banalities like air regulations.

A factor encouraging our attitude was the awe in which Sabres were held by ground controllers. Sabres were always short on fuel. Accordingly, they always gave us priority. We were accustomed to being cleared to descend as soon as we called for it. In fact, it was more of an announcement than a request.

Once, returning to Ottawa over 30,000 feet of clag, the control tower operator crossed me up.

"You'll have to hold on top," he said. "We have an inbound from Montreal."

"How long?"

"Ten minutes."

"Ten minutes!" I exclaimed. "I'm short on fuel."

"Can't help it," said the man.

By this time the radio compass needle was jerking round the dial. It was time to start down. Dive brakes out, throttle to 80%, stuff the nose down. Zunk! Into the clag.

"Why can't you let me down?"

"We have this TCA inbound. You'll have to hold."

"I'll letdown in a different quadrant. How's that?"

"No. You can't do a non-standard letdown."

Down down down in the grey damp murk. Blacker than a cow's inside in there. Check the dials, round and round the shop. Airspeed, horizon, compass, altimeter.

Somewhere below is a TCA something. Viscount? North Star? What about a mid-air collision? Airspeed, horizon, compass—straighten on inbound heading. Down down down. With all this airspace in Canada, is it likely that one iddy-bitty Sabre would prang one airliner? Of course not.

"We'll let you down as soon as we can," the controller says.

Good chap. Rain mashing itself against the windscreen. Altimeter swishes through 5000. Mental note to start looking for the ground at 2000. Airspeed, compass, horizon. The Sword is a great ship for I.F. Steady as a rock. 2000 feet and nothing. Ease up on the descent. We start our patented feeling-for-the-ground technique. Letting down in 200-foot increments.

A rain-swept world appears at 800 feet. Radio compass swings one way, then the other. We see it from the corner of one eye. Ho ho. Clank onto inbound heading.

"Three miles, clear initial," we say cheerfully.

"How did you get down?" Horrified voice.

"Let down visually. Through a hole."

And we chuckled all the way back to the flight room. Nonetheless, the incident brought on a discussion among ourselves. What to do if they told us to hold on top for lower (and lesser) traffic? I trotted out my idea of using one of the other legs of the range and was gratified by its acceptance. The chance came, inevitably, to try it out.

Another autumn day, glowering cloud but no rain, ceiling perhaps 2000 feet. The clag extended to 25,000 feet, also perhaps. Mohawk Black section of four was returning to base and were directed to hold on top.

"We have a TCA North Star inbound at the present time."

"Okay," said Black leader with aplomb. "We'll let-down visual."

"You'll what!"

"Black, dive brakes go."

And down and down they went. Four Sabres in finger formation. Lovely formation. They held it all the way down through 23,000 feet of altostratus. They held it right to that instant when they broke out of cloud and beheld, larger than life itself, a red and white North Star.

"Break!" screamed Black leader.

He said that after everyone in Black section had pulled for their lives. It was a sort of downward Prince of Wales maneuver. Sabres going in every direction. But mostly downward.

Eventually the four Swords congregated, assembling themselves in shaky semblance of a formation. And there was only the trace of a tremor in the voice that announced the news:

"Black is three out with four."

"You're cleared initial, Black. Call the pitch."

The scene—or 'skit' as these things were known—was being related with gestures and shrieks in the flight room, when the telephone interrupted. It was the airport manager. He desired the presence of the pilots of Mohawk Black section in his office. At once.

Four G-suited pilots filed into the office. Standing beside the desk of the senior citizen who was the manager, were two ashen-hued and angry Trans-Canada pilots.

"You nearly rammed me!" said the TCA captain. In essence that is what he said.

The airport manager was a calming influence.

"Hold it, Ted. Hold it. Let's have the story again."

And the TCA captain repeated his horror tale of a sky full of Sabres going in every direction in their efforts to avoid collision with his sacred vessel full of sacred passengers.

So emotional had been the good captain's address, that not a soul in that office was unaffected. The airport manager was quite pale as he turned to Black leader and asked, gravely, what he had to say for himself.

"I didn't see any North Star," said Black leader. "Did you guys?"

No one had.

"I was just flying formation," said Black Two.

"What altitude were you flying?" asked Black Three.

No answer. Indeed, the good captain seemed incapable of answer.

"I think I saw a North Star," admitted Black Four. All eyes were on him as he scrunched his bushy eyebrows in the effort of remembering. "But he was a long way off. Two, three miles." He turned to the airline captain. "Were you flying just below the cloud?"

It was two against four. Four Sabre 'captains' against one TCA captain and his assistant.

I agree. We were very foolish young men.

Sabre 5 flown by Canadair test pilot Bill Kidd out of Cartierville Airport, outside of Montreal, Quebec. Photo was taken by Hugh Mackechnie of Avro Aircraft from the back seat of a T-33. This was one of the first Sabre 5's off the Canadair line. Powered with an Orenda 10 engine, it was comparable to USAF F-86H "Sabre Hog".

Sabre Development

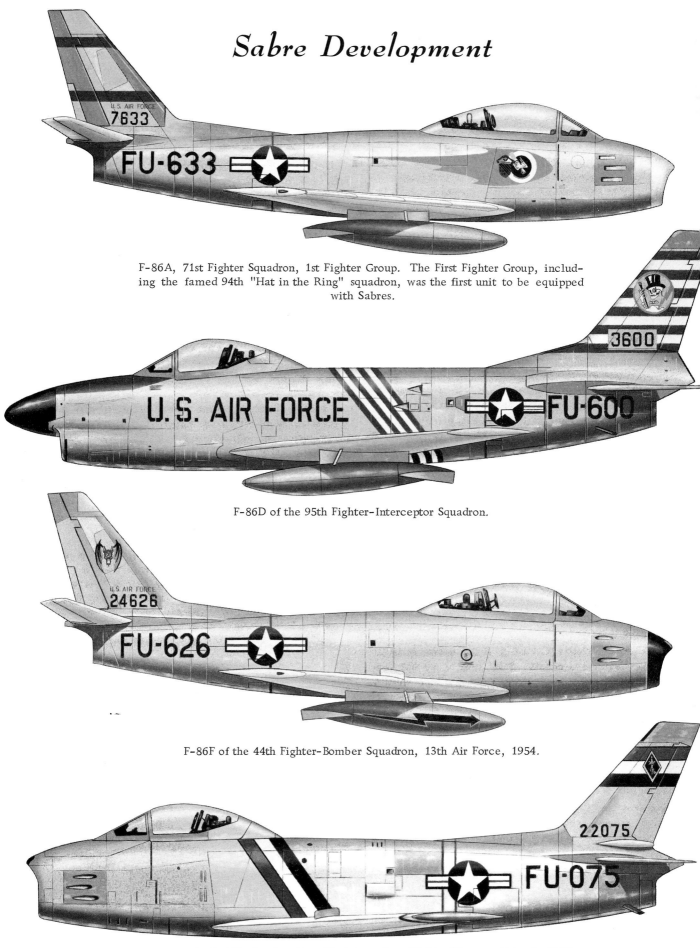

F-86A, 71st Fighter Squadron, 1st Fighter Group. The First Fighter Group, including the famed 94th "Hat in the Ring" squadron, was the first unit to be equipped with Sabres.

F-86D of the 95th Fighter-Interceptor Squadron.

F-86F of the 44th Fighter-Bomber Squadron, 13th Air Force, 1954.

F-86H of the 3595th Combat Crew Training wing, Fighter Weapons School, Nellis Air Force Base, Nevada, 1956.

XP-86A on a test flight over the Mojave Desert, 1948.
(Photo: North American Aviation)

4th Fighter-Interceptor Wing F-86As off on a Mig Alley
sweep, August, 1951. (U. S. Air Force Photo)

F-86D of the 513th Fighter-Interceptor Squadron at Phals-
borg Air Base, France. (Photo: the Menard Collection)

F-86E of the Royal Hellenic Air Force's official aerobatic
team at Buchel Air Base, Germany, 1960. (Photo: the
Menard Collection)

F-86F's of the 4th Fighter-Interceptor Wing's 336th Squadron, ready to depart for Mig Alley. (Photo: North American Aviation)

TF-86F trainer two days before its first flight, on 14 December 1953. This ship crashed three months later during
a test flight. (Photo: North American Aviation)

The F-86H was a beefed-up fighter-bomber version of
the Sabre, equipped to deliver nuclear weapons. (U. S.
Air Force Photo)

F-86K of the French Air Force. "K" models carried 20
mm. cannon in place of the F-86D's rocket armament.
(Photo: the Menard Collection)

The Guns Go Bang

The opportunity to fire the guns was another of those events much looked forward to by the young fighter pilots.

"Trenton for gunnery, chaps."

Station Trenton is on Lake Ontario. It is very old. At the time of which we speak, it was the site of Training Command Headquarters. How much influence this fact had on decisions within our fighter squadron, is difficult to say. But any fighter squadron is apt to hold any training organization in some degree of contempt. Fact of life. Trainers are timid. Well, aren't they?

Ours was the first Sabre squadron to operate from Trenton. To simulate wartime exigencies, we worked out of tents at the end of the long runway. It rained every day. Which was remarkable simulation. Mud, chill and damp. It rained so hard that all the yellow trainer Harvards remained ramped.

"Three hundred feet. Get airborne."

The ceiling had soared to 300 feet.

"What's the viz?" asked this faint-heart.

"Mile'n a half. Go."

Plosh plosh plosh through the mud to the dripping Sabres parked in a row along the edge of the concrete. Grey day. Stratus cloud trailing in the trees. Shivery groundcrew crawl out from beneath the wing to meet their hero the pilot.

"Hit something, will you?" says one.

"Bring it back serviceable," says another.

The air/ground gunnery range was just a few miles away from Trenton. It consisted of square canvas targets set on a driftwood-strewn beach. A small weathered tower stood to one side. Home of the itinerant range officer. That is, the tower was inhabited during gunnery exercises, not simply between attacks.

Plosh plosh plosh round the Sabre. The groundcrew have retreated again to the less-damp area under the wing. From here they discuss their hero.

"What's he looking for?"

"He doesn't know. Let him be."

"Pilots never know. They walk round because someone told them to."

Ignoring their juvenile chatter, we peer importantly into the coal mine which comprises the aft end.

"What d'ya see?"

Laughter. Juvenile laughter. Plosh plosh plosh, carrying on with the pilot's pre-flight external check. There, it's finished. Bend forward to catch the elusive parachute strap and fetch it 'twixt the legs. Snick. Now the other. The audience clamber out from under to assist.

"You're going, huh? All alone? Who's going to lead you back?"

Snick, final chute strap amid the chortles following this allusion to drivers who can't make it back to the runway before running out of gas. As we start the ascent to the cockpit, someone says:

"Did you get the canopy open for him?"

"Somebody did."

More juvenile laughter. We paused, looking into that Sabre cockpit. Water lay everywhere. Especially on the seat where the hollow formed by numberless fat fannies collected the rain. Water dripped and trickled down the faces of the instruments. Someone had forgotten to close the canopy.

"Come on, you guys!"

This expression of discontent evoked an outburst of hilarity. And some advice.

"Sit down. You'll sop up most of it."

The advice was good. That is to say, our advisor was correct. After bailing the surplus water with a scooped hand—flinging it all over the cockpit in our efforts—we sopped up the remainder by sitting. The sensation is not pleasant. One of the groundcrew chaps standing-by on the tarmac shouted encouragement.

"How about starting it?"

"I haven't strapped-in yet."

"Start it first. Strap-in later!"

"Why?"

"We got a stuke game going in the tent. You're holding us up."

It was lonely after they left. Sitting in that moist cockpit, the rain droplets gathering into trickles and then

Bound for the air-to-ground gunnery range with practice rockets are these Sabre 5's of #1 (Fighter) OTU, Chatham, New Brunswick.

Colorado ANG F-86F makes low-altitude run at the USAF Fighter Weapons Meet, Nellis AFB, Nevada, 1955. (U. S. Air Force Photo)

Nellis AFB F-86F passes over targets on low-altitude bomb run at the 1955 Fighter Weapons Meet.
(U. S. Air Force Photo)

slithering along the curved sides of the plexiglass. Comforting was the muffled scream of the idling J-47, and the faint red glow of the instrument lights. Most of the dials were misting over on the inside. We noticed that as we snapped the fastener of our oxygen mask. The rubber was clammy.

"Mohawk twenty-nine, how do you read the tower now?"

"Fives. Take-off clearance."

VHF was temperamental.

"Roger, you're cleared take-off."

Long slow march of the throttle up the quadrant. Tail pipe temp climbs, rpm's wind on, airspeed drum winds up until the needle starts its move. Ahead, slick black asphalt extends into grey nothing. Water splashes, higher, thrashes against the sides and drags at the main-wheels. Airborne. Sabre surges ahead as wheels fold and flaps grind silently up.

Into cloud. Blast. Power back to 80%, poke the nose down to find the grey and rain-drenched world beneath. Altimeter pauses, then starts a slow unwind. At exactly 300 feet AGL, we're visual. Take up a heading of 120. Where's the gunnery range? Already we worry.

A highway slides under, cars with headlights on. Motels with garish lights. Multi-colored tourist cabins. Trailer camp, aluminum cocoons parked in two unimaginative rows. Trees, fields, grey rippled water. Where's the gunnery range? What heading? 120. That's what we're steering. Unlax.

Out of the murk appears a brown sickle of beach. Four white blobs, and to one side a wet wooden tower. Ramshackle. The gunnery range. Congrat's. Call the range officer for clearance onto his range. No answer. His radio must be u/s.

Gentle dive, lining up on No. 3 target. That was the one assigned. Dry run. Chance to arm the guns and set

up your pattern. One more try on the VHF. No joy. White canvas square with 3 painted on it in red flashes under.

Pull up, crank it left, eyes glued to the crescent of sand with its four white dots. There's no sweat using the range without the blessing of the RO. We're only flying one bird at a time today. Fifteen minutes per customer. Pull it! Boot of rudder to keep from falling upwards into cloud.

Hmm. This is going to be a tight circuit. Straighten on a pseudo downwind, roll into the attack before you lose sight of the range. Armament switches on; guns armed. On such a dark day, the gunsight reticle is dazzling. Turn down the intensity. That's better. Now, what other excuses can you find? Tum-te-dum-dum. Like train busters.

Crank it, tight. Gunsight pipper slides across the grey-blue band that passes for horizon today. Let the nose slide down, enough, enough! Pull it. Roll out. Pipper sits four inches above the target. Poke the nose down. Yipe! Pull out. Sudden G drives your fanny into the hollowed seat pack. Climbing turn, neck craning to watch the white blobs on a wet beach. Dumb banana, you didn't even shoot.

Second pass, and this time the pipper stubbornly rests ahead and to one side of the target. A corrective jab of rudder—they say never use rudder—and the pipper slides closer. Not on target. Squeeze the trigger. Brrrt! Like gang busters. And the .5's hose out in deadly lash. A cloud of sand obscures the target as we check back on the pole. The bullets, apparently, go where the gunsight is pointing.

Exhilarated, we go round and round, sometimes getting the pipper on the red 3 on the white square. Brrrt! Brr-rrt! Like train busters in WW II. Like gook-chasers in Korea. Brrrt! The white canvas target rumples and dimples under the storm of sand thrown up on it.

Returning Sabre 5 four-some from the air-to-air gunnery range over the Atlantic not far from RCAF Station Chatham. Instructor and three students make up flight. Gunnery flight Sabres were the only ones flown without drop tanks. Gunnery trips averaged 45 minutes chock to chock.

Clunk - clunk - clunk. The breech blocks clatter emptily.

Ammo expended, time to go home. Quick glance round for FW-190's. None. Sticky smile under sweaty oxygen mask. Pick up a reciprocal heading of 300. Fuel 1000 pounds, fat. VHF to tower freek. No voices. Naturally no voices. You're the only idiot flying at the moment. Next man is probably strapping-in right now. Where's the field?

Unlax. Radio compass booms in loud and clear. Needle points confidently the way you wish to go. Rain obscures the earth, you're belting along in a purplish twilight half-in and half-out of clag. Where's that highway? Unfamiliar trees and fields slide by. Houses, a country church complete with graves, appear and disappear. Worried?

"Trenton tower, Mohawk twenty-nine. Check steer."

No answer. Check the frequency, try again. Try secondary, try distress. A vision of the tower operator downstairs stirring coffee infuriates you. But it isn't him, it's you. While you've been dinking with a duff radio, more landscape has been pouring by. Relax. Use your head.

A moving needle in the dial shop catches your attention. Compass! Check outside, check the artificial horizon, needle-ball. Compass needle turns gently and by itself. Worried? The implications are all there and all at

once. When did the compass go u/s? In the gunnery circuit? Likely. What heading did we really leave the range on? Stand-by compass is completely misted over. It appears to read 350. North?

Fuel 800 pounds. Twenty minutes at this altitude?

"Trenton tower, Mohawk twenty-nine. Do you read?"

Of course they don't read. Or maybe they do, and you're cluttering up the R/T because you sure as heck can't read the tower. Let go the mike button. Now think.

Volume up on the radio compass, check the dial. The station ident's boom-in loud and clear. But why is the needle slowly moving? Is the station over there? Hopefully you turn that way. North. Original heading should have been 300. Little misty compass in the high corner of the cockpit says you went north in the first place. Can't be right. You want so badly to believe that you follow the pointer anyway. A black curtain of rain lies straight ahead. Thunderstorm. The radio compass is homed-in on a thunderstorm.

Turn one-eighty. Sure enough, radio compass swings with it, points straight back. What if the field is back there? What if Trenton is sitting right under that wall of rain? And you can't see it. You stifle the impulse to turn once again. South. Try to back-track to the gunnery range and start over again.

600 pounds fuel. Fifteen minutes?

Sopping green countryside rewinds under us. All the fields appear the same, but aren't. The row of trees, the brown gravel concession lines criss-crossing. A car splashes through a puddle. Lucky sausage. Where's the lake? Where's the sickle beach with the four white blobs? Why did you have to get lost, you dumb prune?

And even as the burning eyeballs scrape away at the horizons, visions of courtmartials dance in our head. With no difficulty whatever, we hear the sonorous findings of the Board: '. . . misuse of available navigation aids' . . . '. . . failed to recognize malfunction of radio and one basic flight instrument' . . . '. . . this accident is assessed as pilot error'.

500 pounds of fuel. How many minutes?

Countryside below. Lots of countryside but no runways. A creek, falling in loops all over itself. Wouldn't it lead to the lake? Eventually? Forget it. But you don't, really, for you jink to the left to follow its winding course.

Pilot error. All accidents can be attributed to pilot error. If nothing else, it was an error for the pilot to climb into the airplane.

Lake shore abruptly appears. Which way? Which way? Keep it to the right, head west. Find the gunnery range. Where is it where is it. Worried? 400 pounds of fuel remaining. When to climb up for the bale-out. Zero pounds of fuel? You need 5000 feet under you. The thought of ejecting in the midst of teeming rain cloud is depressing.

There. The faint brown curve of a beach, waves rippling white along the shore. Turn toward it. Outhouse to one side? Yes! And the four white blobs on the sand. Ignoring now the blessed find below, fasten an eye to the mist-dimmed emergency compass. Turn gently onto 300 degrees. Blast. The thing bobs slowly between 270 and north. Emergency all right.

One minute. Two. A highway and motels.

Out of the mist and murk ahead appears the wet glistening cross of runways. A triangle bisected by the long jet runway. Pick a runway. Any runway you luck sack. Whee!

Gunnery flight Sabre 5's of #1 (Fighter) OTU, Chatham. Diamond-four section on low pass is wearing tanks which was standard for all other OTU Sabres. Students flying wing positions are having trouble holding position.

Surprisingly, there's a whole gaggle of groundcrew standing waiting as you taxi in. What's wrong? D-door hanging? The landing was okay. Their coveralls are black with soak. One of them guides you into the line. Why are they all out here? There are only two slickers to go round.

Set the brakes, throttle round the horn. The J-47 expires. Rain feels cool on your sweaty brow as the canopy grinds back.

One of them climbs up on the wing as you fumble at straps and hoses.

"You get lost?"

"Yeah."

"Figured so."

"How come you guys are so wet?" Hand him helmet and headset.

A trickle runs down from his plastered hair.

"Standing out here listening for your engine." He looks disgusted. "You're a lousy pilot."

Compliment. Groundcrew don't worry about drivers they don't like.

Gunnery flight Sabre 5 over-shooting at RCAF Station, Chatham. Note gear folding, flaps almost retracted.

Germany

Canada's NATO contribution of 12 Sabre squadrons for the defense of Europe was growing. Three squadrons were already in England and the first three for France took off on Leapfrog II across the Atlantic in the autumn of '52. Our outfit was part of Leapfrog III which crossed the Atlantic the following spring for Germany. By that time of course, the squadrons quartered in France were six-month veterans.

The base in Germany was everything that the efficient Germans could lavish on a military base. The French base was everything that the inefficient French could fail to provide. (Sidewalks, heat, doors that opened and windows that closed.)

It might have been the wretched winter they had just survived in the mud of northern France that made the fighter pilots of Gros Tenquin the way they were . . . but I get ahead of my story.

The first few days at Zweibrucken were spent getting settled-in. Naturally, for purposes of NATO propaganda, we were considered "combat ready" the instant we arrived but in actual fact it took a few days to unpack tools and prepare for war. Quite naturally also, our first few flights out of the new base were of the recce variety. A chance to acquaint ourselves with the local terrain, if not the weather. That last took some getting used-to.

"Okay," said flight commander, using the cautionary preceding the executive word of command. "Go!"

The squadron's Sabres were still festooned with the ungainly drop tanks used for the long haul across the ocean.

Sabre 2's of 439 (Fighter) Squadron, over Ottawa, spring, 1952, shortly before 439 and 410 Squadrons transferred to North Luffenham, England. These were the first of twelve Canadian squadrons to serve in NATO Europe.

Sabre 2's of 410 (Fighter) Squadron, RCAF, seen after take-off at North Luffenham, England, summer, 1952. Section leader has chopped power to stay behind photo T-33, Number Two has popped speed brakes. Both Sabres have slats extended, indicating slow forward speed.

"When do we get rid of the tanks, boss?"

"Next week. Now, go."

Flight commanders were so imperious.

We took off in a pair and climbed toward a broken layer of something based about 10,000. The verdant greens of springtime Germany spread out below. Rolling country, wooded hilltops and snaking roads. Villages out of Grimm's. It took a moment to realize that the German farms and fields weren't necessarily laid out on the square. It gave a crazy patchwork pattern to the landscape.

Through the cloud and into trouble.

"Mohawk Green . . ." someone started to say.

There was no time for talking about it. Four silver Sabres were pouncing on us from above. Green leader racked it into a turn, but at climbing airspeed and heavy with fuel. I hate talking about it even.

It wasn't just that they caught us unawares. Or that our combat pair split up almost immediately . . . got split up, that is. Or that we never even got together again. It was just that for the next hour I never saw anyone in front of me. They were all behind. Taking turns taking pictures of me. I couldn't get rid of them!

A neck-cracking turn. But the two silver Swords behind me had no trouble staying with it. Tighter, pull it tighter! The enemy tucked in tighter too. Neck aching from looking over my shoulder. Too green then to know enough to loosen shoulder straps and sit sideways. What to do?

The mental paralysis lasted for awhile, then pride reasserted itself. Weren't we the best pilot in the squadron? Did we tamely accept this? This treatment. We reversed the turn, and now had the pleasure of watching them over the other shoulder.

Scissors! Try scissoring.

So we began a series of shuddering reversals, snapping an already fractured neck-bone first one way then the other to watch the enemy fall away. They didn't fall away. The number Two man pulled up to one side, but the leader calmly followed my frantic gyrations. He had no trouble staying there. Once in awhile I saw his dive brakes flick out to help him on the up side of the balloon. Then he'd slide right back in on my tail.

"Go away!" I shouted into my oxygen mask.

He did, after awhile. He must have run out of camera film. Anyway, he finally pulled up and his Two-man dropped into position behind me. It was a terrible experience. Those two taking turns shooting me down.

Enraged by their over-bearing attitude, I finally flung the Sabre into a spiral dive. Zonk, into the cloud. Through it and into the cool green underneath. Speed building up, the G-load climbing. 4G, tighter. 5G.

"Follow this!" I grunted against the weight. Tears were squeezing out and trickling along the rim of my oxygen mask.

Down and down and down we went. Tighter and

ighter, harder and harder I pulled it. The grey fog of black-out swept into the cockpit. Dimly was I aware of the altimeter unwinding in great leaps, the green countryside swelling toward me. When everything disappeared, I relaxed the pressure.

When sight returned, and sense and feeling, I had—along with two Sabres on my tail—a thumping headache. The sight of those two Sabres in the rear view mirror brought my fighter pilot career to its lowest ebb. What could I do? Except waggle my wings and admit defeat. I waggled. And choked on the crow feathers as the two Swords pulled up alongside.

They had Texaco Red Indian insignia on them. 421 Sqn, based at Gros Tenquin. I wondered, as the leader waved two fingers in traditional obscene gesture, if it was any of my friends. But I never found out. The two broke off and headed for home.

Still with lots of fuel, I set out climbing. Perhaps I had in mind finding Green leader on top of the cloud. We could at least return to base as a pair. And who then, could tell that we'd just been waxed?

Through the cloud and into the dazzling sunlight. With a thumping headache. A beautiful day. Sabre big and alive. Everything, as they say, right with the world. But not for long.

We — the enemy and I — glimpsed each other at the same moment. He was at ten o'clock to me, going to nine and about 2000 feet above. Silver Sabre. Sunlight glinted from his wings as he abruptly rolled into a turn my way.

No you don't, I said. This fight was going to be different. One against one. Him and me. Flying the same airplane, so no one could claim advantages there. It was to be fighter pilot versus fighter pilot. You sausage, I accosted my adversary. And cranked it toward him.

The circle was set up. 4G's on the little clock in the corner. This time I was determined to fly it smooth. To be cunning, adroit, skillful. Mean, aggressive, merciless. All those things that make a fighter pilot what he is. That was me.

Round and round we went. Tighter and tighter became the circle. The sustained G was a burden, weighting the arms, the head and the eyeballs. The inflatable G-suit was crushing my guts up into my chest.

"Ugh!" I groaned into the top portion of my oxygen mask which was sliding down my nose with the G. My opponent was nearly lost in the mists of grey-out.

My pole arm ached, and since the throttle was long-since welded to the firewall, I used both hands on the stick. A familiar crik was developing in my neck and I realized, with despair, that the other Sabre was pulling a tighter circle.

Too soon, too soon I was peering hard over my shoulder at a nose intake and the business end of six point five machine guns. In a few seconds I knew, he'd be shooting film. The thought of being a movie star twice in the one afternoon was too much.

"No!" I squawked and began what, in retrospect, must be termed a hysterical series of maneuvers which I hoped would be evasive.

Rolling, bunting, twisting, looping. Violent scissors, totally unsuccessful. Round and round, up and down, back and forth, to and fro. Banging my head on the canopy trying to see where he was. He was there. Sometimes a little beneath, but seldom to one side or the other, Languidly following my most violent aerobatics. A beautiful toy Sabre, seemingly tied to the tail of my own.

That was the way it went. Through fifteen or twenty minutes and ten thousand feet of altitude. It ended—where prolonged dogfights always end—among the trees. Worthy opponent was still in position behind me. With feelings of deep chagrin and black hatred, I waggled capitulation and throttled back.

Another Red Indian. The insignia of 421 Sqn stood out in bold relief on the shark fin rudder. He formated on my wing briefly. Long enough to wave two fingers then flick a disdainful wing in my face as he flung upwards and away.

How I hated that man.

But that afternoon's humiliations weren't the last. In that spring of 1953 the Sabre jockeys of Gros Tenquin had a field day with the newcomers to Europe. Day after day, it seemed to this witness, I was getting waxed for one reason and another. Mostly ineptitude, I suppose, but certainly not from lack of effort. I hated those GT jockeys with a passion bordering on mania. And I flung myself into every dogfight with a zeal that resembled a death wish.

On the ground, before and after these battles, I lis-

Sabre 5's prior to camouflage edict, circa 1954. Pair believed to belong to 427 Squadron, Zweibrucken, Germany, led by F/L Howie Rowe.

One of the GT boys. . . Sabre 6 of 421 Squadron lands at Gros Tenquin. (Photo: the Menard Collection)

Camouflaged Sabre 6's of 439 (Fighter) Squadron, RCAF, based at Marville, France, 1958.
Camouflage was dirty-brown-and-green top, robin's egg blue bottom.

tened to my companions tell how they had 'hacked' this one or that one. But it seemed to me then, as now, that these dogfights were being won by 'the other guys'. I spent hours trying to sort tactics out of chaos, to recollect moves and counter-moves and their results. Which was well-nigh impossible, for I found the dogfight itself so fraught with terror and alarm, confusion and high excitement, that remembering it afterward was beyond me.

Fighter tactics of WW II were fine, up to a point. But the higher speeds of the Sabres meant a vastly sprawled dogfight. No propeller meant scant acceleration just when you might need it. Loss of airspeed could mean a compressor stall. And high speed pull-outs could mean an over-G. As a matter of cold historical fact, our Sabres were badly bent in these hairy hassles.

But hassle we did. Day after day. The hassles got bigger and hairier as the squadrons began throwing up larger formations. And things got confused after the first clash, for every airplane in the fight was a silver Sabre. You had to be fairly close to make out the individual squadron markings. And if the boys from GT weren't about — which was seldom — we hassled squadron versus squadron.

The swelling hatred I felt for the GT boys was quite capable of turning itself on anyone not in my particular formation. That is, every time I saw another Sabre in the sky, my inferiority complex coupled itself to the raging frustrations of defeats gone by.

It took weeks of humbling before I realized that it was now taking my opponents minutes to get on my tail instead of seconds. Once on my tail, of course, they were usually there to stay. But the intensity of my hate forces reflecting back across my Sabre tailplane probably had its effects. My opponents will live shortened lives.

Anyway, the day finally arrived when something besides defeat was my lot. I was flying number Three in a section led by Sydney, my friend. Twelve Sabres in all, the entire squadron in fact. And we met a like number of Swords near Gros Tenquin and the battle was on. Within seconds our neat sections of four had disintegrated into pairs, and it was everyone for himself and the Two-men hang on for dear life.

There were Sabres going every direction and mid-air collisions were miraculous by their non-occurrence. The radio was a minor bedlam of grunts, curses and G-choked instructions.

"Breaking, Red."

"Pull hard, Four! Harder."

"Got that guy, Al? Turn now. The other way."

At about that time when the mad melee was beginning to split up into writhing segments, I latched onto a Sabre of my own. He was sort of falling past me in the general mix-up and confusion, and since no one was tacked onto my own tail, I half-rolled and got on him. It was wonderful. He twisted and jinked, scissored and yo-yoed. To no avail. I had him wired.

His number Two got lost in the heroics, so did mine. We were alone. Down and down we hassled until finally . . . the inevitable. Among the tree tops of sylvan France: surrender. My prey straightened and waggled.

Extending largesse to a conquered foe is the noble thing to do. And I'm noble. Especially was I noble at the instant of my first victory. I closed the gap between us, pulling up into formation on his starboard wing. How I hoped for a Red Indian insignia.

"Chickenhouse! You idiot."

It was Sydney. My section leader.

Forty Americans Cornered Over Bitburg

It's difficult to know just what the Canadian government was thinking of in those days. Or perhaps that's unfair, since the government was only concerned with providing NATO with 12 squadrons of day-fighter Sabres. And not with what was to be done with them.

The misunderstanding arose from that term 'day-fighter'. The people who led the Sabre squadrons — one CO and two flight commanders — were almost all WW I fighter types. And they thought they were leading fighter squadrons. In the sprogs was inculcated this terrible ethos of WW II: Sabres were fighters and we were fighter pilots.

So we fought. Early and late, coming and going, to or from some mission of forgotten note. The battles usually began in the wild blue of 45,000 feet or whatever the J-47's would give us. Mach was the thing. Keeping up the precious Mach. Stately formations of silver Swords wheeling and turning, wingmen crossing over and under. Everyone flying impeccable battle formation.

Three or four of these ponderous turns-toward-the-enemy were all that patience would allow. One formation leader or the other would throw advantage aside to get the enemy to close.

"Tally-ho!" someone would say.

And the radio discipline went to hell. Orders and acknowledgements, warnings and advice, directions where to look. Cries of triumph and cries for help. And on occasion, when both formations were using the same tactical frequency, jeers and taunts to add to the hubbub. It was wild.

Not half as wild as the battle itself, mind. Round and round, Sabres mixing and re-mixing until nothing remained of the stately formations but struggling pairs.

For the pilot caught in the whirling vortex it was grunt and strain, git or be got. G-force driving you into the seat, pulling at your arms and draining the blood from cranium and eyeballs. But even when the grey mists were closing in from the sides and all that could be seen lay straight ahead, your brain was clear. You could carry on a dialog with yourself.

Banana, you might be saying, you stupid banana. Why did you turn that way? Wonder if Charlie's still with me. Pull! Not too hard. Don't stall. What's the airspeed? Can't look now. Opponents opposite side of circle. Slats banging on the leading edges. Feels okay though. Never knew a Sabre to stall in a turn. Pull! Wing tucks slightly. Don't stall, don't stall!

Pick up an inch on the other's number Two. The gunsight pipper is far down on the windscreen. No hope yet of getting some footage. You wish the other guy would break away. Suffer a mental lapse and reverse his turn. Nobody reverses.

"Green leader." Charlie's choked voice. "Check two at four."

Two somebodies at four o'clock. Neck aches as you swivel it to look in this new direction. Two silver Sabres

about 2000 feet above, half-rolling to carve in on your favorite fighter pilot.

You try to imagine what will happen when you break out of this circle. Four against two. The interlopers are closing fast. Time to do something.

"Breaking starboard, Green."

The Sabre — out of speed and loaded with G — seems slow to answer. The wings feels heavy, the ailerons unresponsive. The white-hazy band that passes for horizon reverses tilt and now you're wallowing in the opposite direction. The attacking pair are reversing too, but they're too hot. You watch their brakes wedge out, and grab the lull in the radio chatter.

"Reverse, Green."

"Rog," says Charlie. Good Two-man that.

Even before your new assailants have slid through your line of flight, you crank the shuddering Sabre back again. The enemy decline the invitation to dance . . . to give up their speed to play games with you. So even though you have them in your windscreen, it's a receding target. They disappear.

Where's the first two? Unable to spot them, you jerk and jink the Sabre trying to see under and behind your tail. Charlie says:

"They went home."

Relief floods through you. Imagine that. They took

Sabre 6's of 441 (Fighter) Squadron, RCAF.
(Photo: the Menard Collection)

European-based F-86F at the 1955 Fighter Weapons Meet, Nellis AFB. (U.S. Air Force Photo)

the opportunity to beat it. You must have been doing better than you figured.

The two of you are alone, even if the radio is still full of the sounds of battle. You scan the sky, looking for someone to bounce. And you grab the chance to check the dials, the oxygen, and fuel remaining. Ten minutes to play.

"Mohawk aircraft return to base."

So it's back to the barn. To sit in the flight room and tell lies and listen to other people's.

One day I had a terrible experience. Like most terrible experiences, it started out innocuous. The weather was CAVU innocuous, the assignment — to test fly a Sabre off a maintenance check — was innocuous.

It was a delightful day as we rolled out on the runway and gleefully fire-walled the throttle. ROAR said the J-47. Rumble rumble rumble said the little wheels under us. Fly said the airspeed needle. Gentle pressure on the pole and . . . airborne. Clunk thunk clunk went the D-doors as the wheels sucked into the wells.

"Off at thirty-one," said the tower.

"Cheers," said the test pilot.

For clipped to my thigh was the card denoting everything about this trip. A record of pressures, temperatures, readings and what-have-you. For the information, edification and enjoyment of the engineering people, I supposed.

As we — the Sabre and I — swept through 10,000 feet and I bent to see what the card demanded for that prosaic altitude, Sam came on the air. My buddy was in trouble. He wasn't admitting that he was in trouble, but that was Sam.

"I got forty Americans cornered over Bitburg."

My left hand was a blur as it pounded the throttle against the stop. Forty Americans. Imagine it. Forty American Sabres . . . Sabre Dogs and Sabre Hogs.

Wheeling and turning in the hot summer sun. Wai for me! Wait for me, I pleaded.

Visions of every Canadian Sabre in Air Division con verging on Bitburg distressed me. Couldn't Sam have been more discreet? Did he have to throw out a genera invitation? Tell everyone? Wait for me, Sam. Hold them for me.

Bitburg was a fair distance away, and I felt sure that entire fleets of Canadian Sabres would already have merged with the 40 Yanks. Nevertheless, a lone coyote might be in time for the crumbs. In time to catch an American falling out of the dogfight, or on the way home for fuel. You know. So I leaned on the poor throttle and compromised best climb for a better ground speed.

This may have been a mistake. In fact, probably was, as things turned out. But then, listening to Sam in the first place was a mistake.

Anyway, I only got to 35,000 feet by the time the silver thread that was the Moselle and the twin airfields of Spangdahlem and Bitburg lying alongside the historic river, slid beneath me. There was no sign of a dogfight. But there were 40 or so Americans. They were all above me.

There must have been some discussion as to who was to have me first. This I deduce years after the event, for how else to explain their odd hesitation? I wasn't sneaking up on them. I might have thought I was sneaking up on them, but I should have known better. Twenty of them tumbled off their perch to gore me.

"Where are you, Sam?" I broke radio silence to ask.

"Oh, I had to go home. I'm about five out."

Five miles from home. Sam. With feelings of deep inner disquiet, I banked gently and straightened to present my attackers with a head-on view. It wasn't this first attack anyway, that was going to get me. It was what was to follow.

Sabre 6 of 441 (Fighter) Squadron, Marville, France, circa 1957.

Sabre 6 of 434 (Fighter) Squadron, Zweibrucken, Germany, 1957.

"Sam," I said. "I'm up here with your Americans."

"They still up there? I'd thought I gave them enough." He chuckled. "Good luck."

My old buddy.

The wild blue was never more wild than it was that afternoon over Bitburg. They were everywhere. Blue-banded Sabres, red-tailed Sabres, yellow-nosed and star spangled ones. Some had drop tanks, some were clean. They were at ten o'clock, three o'clock, six o'clock. All All going for my tail feathers.

Go away, I said, making shooing motions at them. What kind of a skit was this anyway? Forty against one. They should have been ashamed of themselves. An ally too. A loyal Canadian ally. Get away from my tail! CRACK! My skull thudded on the canopy as an iron left leg ramrodded the rudder pedal. Some people say you can't rudder a Sabre round.

Aha! Somebody's stupid number Two slithering across my nose. Get him! Get him! But before I could line up for ten seconds worth of camera-gun footage, it was necessary to take care of something else. Me.

Stretched out behind, in the manner of kite tails and aerobatic teams, were four Sabres. They looked lovely. Out of range, I told myself, but evasive action seemed correct. Back on the pole. Straight up. Blue blue was the sky, speckled with silver. The other twenty Sabres. And starting a loop at 30,000 feet wasn't so smart either.

Nevertheless, the resultant whip-stall and inverted spin certainly shed my pursuers. They all scattered to avoid the mid-air collision as I came tumbling down wing wing. The ultimate maneuver. No one could follow me through on it. Ever.

But of course they were waiting for me to regain mastery of the beast and when things finally sorted themselves out at 23,000 feet, the sky was just as crowded as before. Everyone wanted a piece of me.

The debacle must have lasted twenty minutes. It went on and on. Pesky American allies. Friends. What about that beer party we had for you guys? Sweat trickling down, itching in an eyebrow, over-flowing and flooding an eye with stinging salt. Arm aching, neck broken, stick getting slippery in the palm.

Go on, you guys. Beat it! A whine in that pleading? My tactics were those of desperation too. Violent scissors, vicious reversals which left me canopy to canopy across twenty yards of space with my pursuer of the moment. Swish! The mid-air collision was averted by someone else, not me.

Sickening rhubarb rolls, the tormented Sabre shuddering in a manner which threatened to vibrate the pitot boom free of its wing tip mounting. Slats clanging as we staggered it round on the stall. Is this the way you fly a high sub-sonic fighter?

For the hundredth time, wrench the Sabre high and to the side, fighting for that extra inch of altitude. Two Swords behind, one more sliding in from the near side. He's low. Maybe, just maybe you can . . .

Wallowing Sabre slithers up another fifty feet and flops instead of rolls. High in your canopy, directly overhead in fact, the green earth and a top plan view of a Sabre. Fifty feet below. Closing, as your seven tons of aerodynamic marvel falls.

What to do? The man you are about to collide with peers straight up at death. His Sabre grows, swells to fill the world your windscreen. Nose fading, air sucking through the intake. The paint of the blue band which girdles the Sabre below is scabrous. It's the last thing you recollect seeing as the ailerons bite enough to give you a half-twist going straight down.

Life is that patchwork of greens and dusty browns straight ahead. That misty thread of water called the Moselle lying across the landscape. An airspeed needle passing 400 knots. Yowee! I'll bet he was scared.

The Battle

The time came, inevitably and soon, when the leaders of NATO would conjure up a practice war. It was called 'Operation Coronet' and pitted the forces of southern Europe against those of the north. In the north were the hated British, Belgian, Dutch and American forces in England, while defending the south were the Canadians, French and plucky Americans. I think this is the way it was.

Since both the French and the Dutch were flying clapped-out '84 Thunderjets, and the Americans on both sides flew Sabres, it was decided that the North would paint their wings black and the South would paint their wings yellow. All the pilots could thus tell friendly from foely.

Preparations at our base for this conflict were both serious and secret.

"Is that door locked?" said the moustachioed chief operations officer when all the pilots were crowded into the briefing room. It was. Locked, and checked locked, sir. "Fine. Pay attention, chaps."

And the wing commander went on to explain that the palmy days of our fighter pilotage were over. "You'll be on stand-by, you'll sit at the end of the runway strapped-in ready to punch tits when I give the order from here."

He indicated a mass of electronics, the only recognizable portion of which was a microphone. The C Ops O would direct his battle from where he stood. The points of his moustache trembled with military fervor.

"You'll work out of tents." He paused. We all knew he'd won his DFC in the desert. "They're a lot more operational, anyway."

He pointed out the enemy positions on the wall-size map of Europe. Explained that the American forces in England would defend there. Cautioned us about fuel and warned that if we ran out of gas and were obliged to land at an 'enemy' field, jail and endless interrogation would be our lot.

The C Ops O finished by extracting a long list from an inner pocket. It was festooned with a red tag stamped 'Secret'. He seemed very pleased with it.

"At the present time, you all have your squadron call signs. We change these every few months." He scanned the room for inattention. "Starting tomorrow, you'll get a new squadron call sign every day."

And just to confuse things further, he added that our control tower — and all the other friendly control towers where we might want to land — would change their call signs every day too.

"And if you don't know the correct call sign, gentlemen," the C Ops O glared. "The control tower will not answer you."

It sounded operational enough for anyone.

The next morning found our squadron operating out of a couple of tents at the end of the runway. At the other end of the runway was another squadron. Our Sabres were lined up along the edge, sort of pointing in the direction of take-off. Presumably theirs were too. The possibility of mid-runway collisions was obviated by the use of different call signs. And, we were assured, only one squadron would be scrambled at a time.

Dawn came somewhere about 6 o'clock. We'd been out there since five. A line of ghostly Sabres parked silent and ready, four of them with pilots sitting strapped-in. Beside the first two were electrical power units for starting the Sabre engines. The squadron only had two

Sabre 6 of 439 Squadron, RCAF, based at Marville, France, 1958.

Pilots of 434 (Fighter) Squadron, RCAF, sitting out by the end of the runway on "alert" status watch a 12-plane belonging to 427 (Fighter) Squadron fly by for the camera man, summer, 1954. Pilots, left to right: Flying Officers Henry Smith, Pete Cunningham, Al Hunter, Fred Allport and Syd Burrows.

APU's. To one side stood a tall steel stake from which hung a loudspeaker.

At seven o'clock, the first four pilots crawled stiffly down and were replaced. We were Peacock Purple section, I was Purple Two. The only good thing about that call sign was that tomorrow it would belong to some other outfit. Carefully I strapped-in and, since I had an APU plugged into me, checked all those things that are checkable such as trims. We were to sit in the cockpits for two hours and if we hadn't been scrambled by that time, change pilots.

Yawn.

The chilliness of pre-dawn and the coolness of dawn gave way to summer heat. By eight o'clock the cockpits were sweatboxes. Our aircraft were pointing eastward and that meant looking into the full blaze of the sun. There was no where to hide your head, which was the only movable portion of your immobile anatomy. On the projecting lip of the front windscreen perched crash helmet and inner headset.

Yawn. It was hot and sweaty and boring. A numbness of the backside set in. Two hours of waiting. For what? A squadron of British Canberras zooping in over the hill to 'destroy' our base? It was the one thought that could stimulate.

But by the end of the second hour, nothing could stimulate. I was hot, numb, irritable, cheesed-off and disgusted with a war only a few hours old. As the clock in the corner ticked away the final minute, and my replacement stood up from the shade under the wing to buckle his 'chute, I unfastened everything. Shoulder harness, parachute, oxygen hose . . . every last hot clinging encumbrance to ventilation. I stood up in the seat.

"SCRAMBLE PEACOCK PURPLE! SCRAMBLE! SCRAMBLE!"

It was the C Ops O's loudspeaker hanging on the post.

When the bugle sounds the clarion call to battle, one always supposes that one will be ready.

Amid shouts of abuse from senior officers there to witness the start of war, the groundcrew and my fellow waiting pilots, I sat down. The lights in the cockpit were all aglow signifying that the APU was ready even if the driver was not.

There were the shouts, as I said. The roar of the APU's, the caterwauling of the loudspeaker which was spewing directions in a most war-like manner.

". . . . climb to angels thirty on a heading of one-two-zero, patrol line Baker, contact Camel Operations channel twelve after airborne. Scramble, scramble!"

What to do first? Straps? Oxygen hose? Hard hat? Radio plugs? The grinding of Peacock Purple leader's J-47 frightened me. I became aware of the shouts of faithful groundcrew chappie standing by my APU.

"Start the bloody thing you prune!"

Yes yes by all means, yes. How do you start it? The rpm's were grinding on . . . 7% . . . 8 . . . 9%. Poom! went the leader's engine. Without waiting for the requisite number of rpm's for start, I flexed the throttle to throw the fuel round in the pots and flipped the switches. POW! Tail pipe temperature soaring. Leader was rolling out.

The groundcrew were already snaking the APU out of the way so I stamped on the brakes to release them and poured the throttle up the quadrant. Purple leader was tilting dangerously as he skittered to aim

These Sabre 5's presumably belonged to one of the RCAF's NATO Europe squadrons.

down the runway. With my own rpm's winding round the clock toward 80%, through 80 to 85%, I skittered and tilted even more chasing him. The crash helmet tumbled off its perch into my lap. I backhanded it into the rudder well and sought to get out of the wind by thumbing the canopy switch.

Zunk! Canopy closed. Leader was 30 yards ahead, black smoke pouring from the charcoal rimmed orifice. It felt strange belting down a runway with no straps done up and no helmet or headset. Purple lead jumped into the air so I did too. What next what next? Wheels! In a convulsion of memory I ripped the little lever through its 'combat' position to 'up'.

Then, panting with the whole gamut of emotions — fright mostly — I drew bead on the leader's tailpipe and organized my thoughts. All the straps were undone. The parachute leg straps were bunched securely under my fanny. I made mental note not to bale-out and ignored parachute straps. Similarly with the shoulder harness. The straps were behind me, so I left them there. The lap strap I fastened.

Communication with anyone was impossible without a hat, so I quickly donned headset and bone dome. I even remembered that it was necessary to plug in the jack plugs which connected pilot to radios. Finally, and to prove that I was not panicky or even confused, I remembered to fasten the oxygen hose.

The fact that I didn't hear anything on the radio didn't bother me. Hadn't the C Ops O warned us about maintaining radio silence?

The rich amber glow of a warning light bathed the cockpit and me in its garish illumination. My heart stopped. Then thudded painfully as I recollected that amber lights advise of situations, while red lights announce disaster. I leaned ahead to read the inscription beside the glowing light. 'Gear'.

Gear what? Gear unsafe? Gear half-way up? Nose-wheel hanging? A D-door about to be torn off with my excessive speed? 220 knots said the airspeed. About 20 knots faster than limits. 230 knots, 240. The amber light continued blazing in my face. I winced listening for the sound of rending metal. The clatter of D-doors being ripped away.

Unable to stand the uncertainty any longer, I broke radio silence.

"Purple leader, Two here. I got a gear warning light."

"What color?"

"Amber."

Even as I said it, I realized my error.

"Put your gear handle to 'combat'."

The amber light always stayed on until the handle was lowered to that intermediate position.

"Peacock Purple Two," said a biting British voice in my headset. "This is Camel Operations."

I replied nothing, content to shrivel quietly there in the cockpit. It was the C Ops O.

"You — bungling — fool! Report to my office when you land."

The patrol, aside from that, was uneventful.

First Kill

The first few days of the war were boring. For some reason or other, (our military leaders seemed vague about it themselves) we were sent out on patrol much as Guynemer and the lads did forty years since.

"You will patrol on a line between Trier and Nancy," the C Ops O was apt to say, "and attack military aircraft only."

One might have thought the skies of West Europe to be swarming with airplanes. And perhaps they were, but never at 40,000 feet between Nancy and Trier.

Our patrols went out and our patrols came back again. No one saw anything. The squadron at the other end of the runway was charged with 'aerodrome defence' and they at least had chased some marauding Canberras. I believe, in fact, that our base had been 'obliterated' early in the exercise by these low level English artists but in the interest of keeping the war going, the umpire at our base allowed us to continue in business.

It was a case of waiting in a Sabre cockpit for a scramble call that never came, or waiting on a slippery tin chair for your next chance to wait in the cockpit, or waiting at 40 or 45,000 feet for an enemy to appear. None ever did.

This waiting game extended from 5 am until 10 at night, or whenever the last vestige of daylight was gone. It made for a long day.

The patrol line itself was a crashing bore. I guess they always were, and it's true that the heroes of the Battle of Britain spent many more hours crawling the patrol lines than they did repulsing the Hun. But no one had told us that. We were left to discover for ourselves one of the true hells of war: flying the patrol line.

It was all psychological, of course. But again we didn't realize it at the time. The affair started out at high pitch of excitement, then went through successive stages of disllusion, frustration, boredom and finally ennui.

After waiting all morning for the chance to sit waiting in the cockpit for the chance to go flying, imagine the excitement of:

"SCRAMBLE BULLDOG RED, SCRAMBLE SCRAMBLE!"

And as our sweaty little forefingers stabbed at toggle switches in the corner, and the J-47's ground through the first stages of start, the loudspaker finished the rest of it.

Climb two-five-zero, angels forty-five, patrol line Able. Contact Clambake channel twelve."

Or something like that.

Anyway it was hustle hustle, wind 'em and go. Four Swords pelting down the runway, smoke belching, nosewheels extending as the pilots took the weight off. Lifting, or bounding, or drifting into the air. A scuffling for position and the leader already bending it round to the climb heading of 250 degrees.

The excitement was still there as the formation finger four struggled for altitude. Everyone wondering if the attack had begun. If the hordes from the North had started down. If radar had a paint on a flight of B-47's from England. Or hairy air battle involving other squadrons was in progress and we were rushing like Blucher to Waterloo.

"Channel twelve, Red," directs the leader.

Everyone lets go the stick long enough to flick the VHF selector the required number of stops. Faint-hearts steady the pole with the left hand.

"Clambake, Bulldog Red."

"Roger, Red. How many chicks?"

"Red with four."

"Rog', make angels forty-five."

Echelon Sabre 6's of 434 (Fighter) Squadron, Zweibrucken, Germany, 1957. 434 Squadron's emblem is the Bluenose sailing ship.

Sabre 5 of 439 (Fighter) Squadron landing at Zweibrucken, Germany, 1954.

"You got some business for us, Clambake?" Hopefully.

"Negative. Call established patrol line Able."

That was when the disillusion set in. Disgusted, Red leader waves his hands outwards and the formation obediently spreads into 'close battle' for the climb. At the top, they spread a little more into ordinary 'battle'.

Practically the last radio transmission for the trip is when Red leader announces to the radar controller:

"Red at forty-five starting patrol line now."

Back and forth they go, pounding a beat between Metz and Luxembourg. The only relief to tedium the cross-over turns at either end. After forty-five minutes of this, or whenever fuel reserves dictated, they leave the patrol line for home.

On one occasion, your correspondent was flying number Three in such a formation. A hot humid day with thunderstorms and towering cu' infesting the thick blue haze of the industrial Saarland. The earth was a murky blur as the sun began to fade. We flew the patrol line by radio compass. Finally the leader called leaving our patrol.

"Peppermint Red is heading for homeplate."

So we kept our battle formation of two and two, and started a long descent for home. At 30,000 we were among the cathedral spires of cloud which, by 25,000 feet, obscured the sun and left us in murky limbo, a twilight zone of haze and shadow. Now and then the leader and his wingman were lost to view behind cloud castles.

It was at one of these moments when Red Two announced:

"Bandit at nine o'clock."

The radar operator was quicker on the mike button than either me or Red leader.

"Investigate! Investigate!"

"Roger." Red leader's voice was a calming influence at a time when calm influences were hard to find. "Red One and Two going down for a look. Red Three, you check?"

"Roger," I muttered, already racking it to where I'd last seen Red One and Two.

A lone bandit, sneaking through the cloud tops. Gone was the ennui, the creeping boredom and disillusion. Here was battle. My heart was thumping despite the massive constriction in my chest. Pop . . . we were through the cloud spire which had separated us from them.

Below us, perhaps 10,000 feet below, a tiny black plane. It seemed to skulk among the cloud tops, flitting from cloud pile to cloud pile. Heading for Paris, by the look of it. An atom carrier? Red One and Two were dropping away toward the bandit. The luck sacks. I hoped that Red leader would give us a crack at it.

"Okay," said Red leader's voice unexpectedly. "It's a civil airliner. Red is breaking off left."

Disappointment flooded through me. I saw the two dinkey-toy Sabre silhouettes curve away from the atom carrier, and turned that way too. The radar controller answered him.

"Did you get the type and registration?"

"Negative. Red Three, could you get that information?"

Heaven sent chance. Divinities smiling on young fighter pilots. I half-rolled and began a joyful pull. The radar controller had premonitions.

"Red Three?" he said.

"Red Three investigating," I said importantly. And half-rolled out again before going supersonic.

"Use NATO procedure."

What NATO procedure. Gunsight switches on, wingspan bar over to 'big'. The prey was growing larger. I carefully judged the pursuit curve. Curves of pursuit are much favored by gunnery officers but I often thought you'd do better from directly behind.

"Red Three?"

"Roger, check that."

But the man wasn't satisfied. Even as I was wondering whether to use the speed brakes now or later, and was busy pulling the light reticle on the windscreen up onto the enemy, he began quoting the regulation.

"You will formate on the aircraft to be identified at a distance of not less than two thousand yards, from which position the pilot will ascertain the type, identity, nationality and registration of the unknown aircraft, as well as noting the direction and speed of flight with regard to possible destination and at the same time endeavor to determine whether the unknown aircraft's purpose is hostile to any or all of the NATO member countries."

Two miles now from the victim, dead line astern.

Closing like clappers.

"Brakes," I said to my wingman, and flicked the switch on the throttle.

The Sabre pitched once, bucked, and then settled down again as the big boards on the sides reached full extension. As a hundred unwanted knots disappeared, I clicked the switch again and sucked them in. About now I'd have been shooting. Big airplane getting bigger in my gunsight. Heinkel, Dornier . . . any of the bad guy bombers we Allies had ever fired on. Brr-rrt go the guns.

Big BIG AIRPLANE. Yowee! Vertical pull up, slow roll on the way. Pull it inverted across the victim's unscathed whale-like back. You great big hunk of junk. The radar man is calling.

"Have you identified the unknown yet?"

"Rog'." Push the excitement from the voice. "An Air France DC-4."

"Did you get the registration?"

I glance across the sky at my wingman who's now tucked in close. He's laughing and gestures one hand like a duck. I should answer.

"From two thousand yards how do you expect me to get any registration?"

"Okay, Red Three. Check an Air France DC-4."

Due to an over-developed sense of honesty — Red leader's — I was unable to claim my first kill.

F-86F of the Argentine Air Force.
(Photo: North American Aviation)

F-86F of the Chinese Nationalist Air Force.
(Photo: North American Aviation)

Sabre Mk. 32 of the Royal Australian Air Force.
(Photo: Brian Baker)

Sabre 6 of Jagdgeschwader 71, Federal German Air Force.
(Photo: the Menard Collection)

F-86D of the Japanese Air Self-Defense Force. This ship
formerly belonged to the USAF's 40th Fighter-Interceptor
Squadron. (Photo: the Menard Collection)

F-86F of the Royal Thai Air Force.
(Photo: the Menard Collection)

F-86F of the Royal Norwegian Air Force.
(Photo: the Menard Collection)

F-86D of the Royal Danish Air Force.
(Photo: the Menard Collection)

Korea...1950-1955

F-86A of the 4th Fighter-Interceptor Wing. First Sabre unit to arrive in Korea, the 4th flew its first operational sorties on 17 December 1950. The black and white fuselage and wingtip bands soon gave way to the standard yellow and black which was applied to all Far-East based Sabres.

F-86E of the 51st Fighter-Interceptor Wing. The 51st converted from F-80's to F-86's in the autumn of 1951 and became the second unit to fly the Sabre into combat, beginning operations on 1 December 1950.

The 8th Fighter-Bomber Wing converted from F-80's to F-86's and took its Sabres into combat on 8 April 1953.

F-86F, Osan, Korea, 1955. The 18th Fighter-Bomber Wing traded its aging P-51's for Sabres during the early months of 1953 and flew its first operational F-86 sorties on 25 February.

Captain Lonnie R. Moore flew this F-86F with the 4th Wing's 335th Squadron.
He finished the war with ten victories. (Photo: North American Aviation)

18th Fighter-Bomber Wing four-some taxiing out for a mission from Osan.
(Photo: North American Aviation)

On the next two pages artist Richard Groh shows elements of #2 Squadron, South African Air Force, joining up for the return flight to Osan after an uneventful patrol of Mig Alley, during the Korean War. This squadron was attached to the American 18th Fighter-Bomber Wing and carried the Wing's identifying red, white, and blue tail stripes.

The Hat Trick

The number of fighter pilots in the world who can claim three confirmed kills during a single sortie is limited. They are, to coin a cliche, rare birds. Without bothering to examine the common characteristics shared by these men — aggressiveness, consummate skill, cunning, etc. — it is necessary to chronicle the bare event. History is, after all, bigger than all of us. And it is for the sake of history that your correspondent records the hat trick scored by himself low in the skies over France.

Low in the skies is correct, for the warlords of NATO changed our squadron's role from high level to low level. This was a welcome change. We had yet to meet an enemy along the patrol lines at 45,000 feet. Excitement was running high when the C Ops O broke the news to us that evening. And he finished up with:

"You start tomorrow. Official dawn is 0520 hours, you'll take-off at 0500. You'll rendezvous with a French fighter-bomber force of '84's over the abandoned airfield at Erize . . ." indicates on wall map . . . "at 0520. You will escort them to Brussels and back. Questions?"

"Yes sir. What about fuel?" '

"Will you have enough? No." Pause for effect. "You'll land at Bitburg. The Americans are expecting you."

Rendezvousing at the exact moment of official dawn was deuced clever.

The escort mission was big. It was to take our entire squadron and accordingly twelve Sabres were readied for dawn. Twelve Sabres, divided into three sections of four — Red, Yellow and Blue sections. I was to lead Yellow.

The screams in the inky blackness of the tent at 4:30 am were occasioned by the acts of dragging clammy G-suits over warm gooseflesh. Minutes later we were stumbling over stray chocks and tin chairs on our way way to the hulking Sabre silhouettes. Muffled cries and curses. Wet legs in the dew-sodden grass.

Even waiting in the cockpit was cold and shivery.

Wing Commander Fred Mills, C. O. of 411 (Fighter) Squadron, RCAF Auxiliary, leads F/L Army Hollinsworth on low pass across ramp at Station Downsview, Toronto. Canada's Auxiliary Squadrons in Montreal, Toronto, and Vancouver were equipped with Sabre 5's between 1956 and 1958. Photo by Barry Herron, May, 1958.

There was no sign of dawn. Of course, it was 2! minutes away. At exactly 24 minutes from dawn and rendezvous, the CO started engine. The rest of Red section fired-up, then it was our turn as the groundcrew brought the APU's and plugged them in. As I got my flame, I noticed Red section taxiing out. Mostly by noise, for navigation lights weren't allowed.

Gingerly I followed the four black shadows trundling down an unseen taxi path to an equally unseen runway It was better when I got behind them, for the small orange circle of fire up their respective flues, was almost as good as nav lights.

"Matador Red, take-off."

The day's call sign was Matador. It was confusing changing it each day.

"Roger, cleared take-off. The time is zero-one."

One minute late. And still black as a cow's insides. Afraid of losing sight of Red section, I rolled out on the runway behind them and careless of the buffeting thunder of their jetwash. My wingmen were there too.

"Red rolling."

"Yellow, take-off," I asked.

"Roger, Yellow, you're cleared."

The little orange circles receding down the runway were becoming smaller as I poured the throttle open and urged myself airborne. They were orange dots of light as we pulled wheels. Four orange specks disappearing in a purple murk that was cloud and darkness together. Of official dawn, there was no sign.

Heavily I leaned on the throttle and glued my eyeballs to the four orange specks ahead. If I lost sight of Red leader . . . why hadn't someone mentioned at briefing that we'd be taking-off in the dark?

Dark? It was blacker than a cow's insides. I said that. Well it hadn't got any lighter. Maybe Red leader would think to throttle back so Yellow and Blue could catch up.

At that instant, at 500 feet, in darkness, over unknown terrain, a horrible red glow suffused the cockpit. My cockpit.

FIRE WARNING.

They say that in those extreme moments, the ones when your parachute doesn't open like, that you will remain calm and even view the scene in a detached manner. This is true. There were two fire warning lights in the Sabre cockpit, one atop the other. If the forward fire light came on, you baled at once. If it was the aft fire warning light, you paused before baling.

The blinding red glare was emanating from the aft warning light. Ascertaining this even as I wrestled with the lock wires of the seat handle, I paused to consider the proper course of action. First of all, I reasoned, some-the proper course of action. First of all, I reasoned, some-one should be notified. In case I baled before it blew, or it blew before I baled. This thought was not pleasant. So I notified the CO of my predicament and my course of intended action.

Sabre 5's of 401 (Fighter) Squadron Auxiliary over home city of Montreal, spring, 1958. 401 Squadron is the most famous of all Canadian fighter squadrons, the only one to take part in the Battle of Britain.

"My fright red fryer warning light is on!"

And while eleven other Sabre drivers turned snow white, I yanked the throttle back to 80% and the stick back to get some altitude. The light went out. There was no fire. The surrounding darkness terrified me and I had lost my section. Down with the nose again. Miraculously, I fell amid my wingmen. They didn't appear to have missed me.

"Who said that?" squeaked the CO, finding his voice.

No one answered.

"Is someone in trouble?" the CO asked more firmly. Still no answer. I had another problem anyway. The four orange lights of Red section had disappeared.

"Red leader," I said in careful accents. "Yellow leader here. I've lost you."

Yellow leader all right. I should have asked for a different color.

"Okay, Yellow lead," said CO cheerfully. "Carry on to the rendezvous."

"Blue checks the same."

Blue leader was lost too.

So I carried on to the abandoned airfield at Erize. Found it, too. It was recognizable in the early early light as a large open area with two small hangars to one side. I throttled right back and set up a smooth orbit to port. The time was 0521 hours. No sign of the bomber fleet, and no sign of Red section.

"Yellow is orbiting the rendezvous," I announced.

"Keep your eye open," replied the CO. "Red section is orbiting too. Have you seen the bombers?"

My hackles rose and I noticed my wingmen bobbing up and down with fear as we tried to pierce the gloom for another section of Swords. We were all alone. Blue leader came on the air, a plaintive note in his voice.

"Well I'm orbiting the rendezvous, but I don't see you guys."

At five in the morning France, it appears, is filled with abandoned airfields.

"Has anyone seen the bombers?" the CO repeated.

No one answered. Round and round we went, searching the gloom and the patches of ground fog beginning to form on the slumbering earth beneath. 0525 hours came, as did 0530 hours.

"We'll wait ten more minutes," the CO decreed from his abandoned airfield. "They must be late."

It was useless, of course, though it is only fair to state that the suggestion that the French bomber fleet might be late did not strain our credibility.

At 0540 hours, as the forward visibility increased to two miles, the CO directed:

"Okay Yellow and Blue sections, join me over at this field."

No one laughed. Not over the R/T. But no one answered, either. So the CO finally said:

"Okay, Matador formation, set heading for Brussels. We might be able to pick up the bombers."

So away we went, pouring along at 1000 feet over a mist-shrouded European countryside all but indiscernible by dawn's early. Not that we were looking at countryside, we had spread out in battle formation and were looking for our charges, the French fighter-bombers. Overhead — perhaps at 4000 feet — was a layer of cloud. So we were bumbling our way in a murky half-light between layers. And seeing nothing.

It went on quite awhile that way. Suddenly the R/T silence was broken by a shout:

"Bandits! Over there."

"Where?" came the CO's voice. And: "Who is this?"

"Red Four, sir. I saw something."

"Where?"

"At nine o'clock. Going to seven."

"Going to seven? That's the wrong way."

The CO meant it was the wrong way for our French fighter-bomber fleet to be going. But of course, and this thought leapt into everyone's mind including the CO's, it could be an ENEMY fleet attacking us!

"Tally-ho!" cried the CO.

And all the rest of us were left vainly scouring the greyish murk. Somewhere, and not many miles from where Yellow section flew, was a dogfight. Bitter thought. Lucky sacks in Red section. Why couldn't it have been us? Why? Why? The CO came on the air again.

"It's no use, we've lost them. Yellow and Blue sections, keep your eye open for an enemy force."

Please, don't let Blue section see them first. Without taking my straining eyeballs from the windscreen, I reached way down and flipped on the gunsight. And I saw the enemy. A few at first, but then more and more of them stretching away into the haze. Serried ranks of them and I felt like Raleigh counting Spanish galleons. A whole Armada. And they were heading right for our bases.

We were broadside to the enemy, and a thousand feet below. I waggled, and Yellow section closed up. Everyone had seen the breath-taking sight. And it was that. Magnificent mass formation flying, diamond fours and tucked-in tight. F-84's, as we swept closer. Probably the rascally Dutch.

As I pulled up to the cloud base and half-rolled to start down, I broke the news.

"Red leader, Yellow here. I've got the formation in sight."

And I was about to add that I couldn't see the black wings which belonged to the forces of the North yet. In fact, I was telling myself that they must be yellow wings because they weren't showing up against the silver sides, when the CO roared:

"ATTACK! ATTACK!"

There it was. A direct order.

"Spread out, Yellow. Each guy take a diamond."

Line astern and closing fast. Ahead, the imperturbable fleet of F-84 bombers. Oblivious to all except their fantastic ability to fly close formation.

I took the rear-most diamond, fondled the slot-man in my sight, blasted 10 seconds worth of camera film at him then slid it up ahead to get the Three-man. When his wingspan filled my world I checked forward on the pole, then back as the diamond four flashed overhead. Straight up in front of the leader.

It was fantastic. They all had yellow wings. Our French allies. The bomber force we were to escort. Either they were returning early, or they were lost and heading the wrong way. As it turned out, the first guess was correct. But that isn't what was fantastic.

The armada disintegrated. Exploded. In the space of a single instant it went from orderly procession to chaos as leaders sought to ram their wingmen and wingmen sought to lose their leaders. There were '84's going straight up, and '84's going straight down. One intrepid chap continued straight ahead, slow rolling through a sky full of death. Fantastic.

And, half-ashamed of the deed, and afraid to venture back into the maelstorm of '84's, I continued on into the cloud deck above. It was only a few thousand feet thick and I popped into the rosy dawn-lit blue above.

The sun was just cracking the horizon. One, two and finally, three Sabres with me. The CO was calling me.

"Yellow leader, did you contact the enemy?"

"Roger."

"What were they?"

"'84's." I smirked into my oxygen mask. "Where are you going now?"

"We'll rendezvous at Bitburg. You check that Blue?"

"Blue leader."

So we set sail for the American base at Bitburg. I took about 20 minutes which left us about 10 minutes of fuel. Which would have been fine except that as we arrived, the rascally Dutch were attacking Bitburg with F-84's. The tower controller warned us about it before we got there.

"The field is presently under attack," he said calmly. "Here comes one now. Yow!"

As one man, Yellow section stuffed the noses down. We were heading due west.

"Where are the '84's now, Bitburg?" Red leader asked.

"They're attacking north to south."

"Okay. My section is coming in from the south."

Red from the south, me from the east. Where was Blue?

"Bitburg, Blue leader here. Ten miles west your base. Where is the enemy now?"

"They're coming in from the north." The controller's voice rose. "About ten miles. I can see them!"

I was about 10 miles, with Yellow section spread out in battle, going like clappers in the dive. If I were closer to Bitburg than either Red or Blue, I could head the Dutch off right over the field.

"Red leader is at ten miles. I don't see the enemy."

"Blue section ten miles."

Everyone was at 10 miles.

Level over the trees now. Tin hangars ahead. 530 knots on the clock. Where are the Dutch? I strained my eyes looking for the enemy to appear from the right. What a surprise for them, I thought.

As we cleared the airport boundary I saw them.

At least 16 F-84's, and all of them in a gaggle. Odd way to attack an airfield. Perhaps the Dutchmen thought our method of attacking them odd too. The American tower operator was the only sane man in the lot.

"You Sabres break!" he screamed. "Break!"

But it was too late. Three sections of Sabres merged with four sections of the enemy at grass-top height over Bitburg. It was hell.

The Dutch leader and I were about to collide. Feeling certain that he would pull up, and wanting him to feel free to do so, I snuggled closer to the grass. Stubborn people, the Dutch. He refused to pull up. Beyond was the row of tin hangars, growing larger. So was the '84. Pull up you sausage, I encouraged him mentally.

Death isn't so bad. I mean, all those terrors they talk about.

"Break!" the tower operator continued to shout.

When you're two feet off the infield you don't break. You squeeze rudder to steer yourself between the hangars. That's where I met Blue section. A head-on. But since Blue was at 20 feet I had room underneath. In the clear again, I found my voice.

"Yowee-e!"

And we went straight up. Yellow section was on the top of the loop at 10,000 feet. Directly under us lay somnolent Bitburg. Not an airplane in sight. Had the Dutch fled? Did we give them such a fright that they'd logged off for home?

"The eighty-fours are coming back again!" announced the tower operator.

That's one thing about the Dutch.

"Dive brakes, Yellow," I said.

This time the Dutch split their force and attacked Bitburg from different directions. Down down we plummeted, but this time with the speed brakes dragging and throttles back. A section of '84's appeared beneath just turning in for another ground strafing attack. We picked them up and followed them in.

The new battle that ensued over Bitburg was harsh and bitterly fought. The Dutch used their shorter turning radii to dart and dodge among the hangars, attempting to scrape pursuing Sabres off on whatever projection they could. The Sabres for their part tried to stay below and behind the artful Dutch. It was a great show.

The owners of the place showed up, American Sabres returning to Bitburg from a raid of their own.

"You can't land here!" the tower told them. "The field is under attack."

"Who's attacking?" American leader wished to know.

"Dutch eighty-four's. You'd better land elsewhere."

"No, man. I'm three out for a straight-in."

"You can't! It's dangerous."

And it was. Skirmish after skirmish was taking place below circuit height and within the confines of Bitburg Air Base. But the American leader was adamant.

"I'm on a flame-out approach now, Man."

"Is this an emergency?"

"Well, what do you think!"

Then a terrible thing happened. Even as the tower operator was busy clanging bells and other vital actions associated with emergencies, and pleading for everyone to clear the circuit, the American leader was asking:

"Bitburg? Have you got something else 'sides old eighty-fours round here?"

"Roger. Some Canadian Sabres."

Silence. Then:

"Will you tell one of them to get off my tail so I can land?"

And lucky for the rest of us that the Dutch decided to vacate the premises just then, for we were all short of fuel. Everybody landed at Bitburg, but we didn't get to talk to any American fighter pilots.

A day or two later, back at our own base once more, an Intelligence Officer came bustling into our dispersal tent. He was waving a reel of gun camera film.

"Great!" he said. "It's great! The umpire says it's the best air-to-air film of the war." He paused in his gesticulations to point at me. "Chickenhouse got three kills! Two eighty-fours and a Sabre with its wheels down."

Uncamouflaged Sabre 5, probably stationed at Baden Soelingen, Germany, over the Alps.

Fly-Pasts

If the career of a wartime fighter pilot is reckoned in op's, or tours of op's, the career of a peacetime FP is reckoned in fly-pasts. For there is nothing more beloved by military Brass, politicians, or air show committees than majestic flights of jet fighters pooping by in impeccable formation. The larger the better.

The moguls of NATO are no different and the skies of western Europe resound to the thunder of jet engines as someone somewhere is being impressed by our military might.

The mechanics of a fly-past vary but little. Someone is appointed fly-past master. Someone else — the less senior the better — is appointed to lead the gaggle. The number of aerodynes involved is a function of the importance of the personage or occasion. ie: the Queen, or the Paris Air Show, would qualify for a maximum effort.

For the individual pilot, nothing much is required except his presence at the briefing. This is always conducted in a room too small for the number of pilots. Once everyone is jammed in, the doors are bolted and cigarettes lit.

"Pay attention, chaps," the fly-past master is apt to say. "Let's have a time hack."

Everyone synchronizes chronometer. A very formal atmosphere prevails through this ceremony, even though nobody's watch but the formation leader's will be used. However.

". . . four, three, two, one hack!"

The FPM walks to map illustration of fly-by route. It is becoming difficult to see him from the back of the room. He is wielding a pointer.

Fly-by of early Sabre 2's of No. 1 Fighter Wing, RCAF, then based at North Luffenham, England, 1952.

"Punch tits at one-three, gentlemen, I want everyone airborne by twenty. Got that?"

People write with ballpoint on their hands. The start engines time joins the radio freeks written there.

Tap-tap-tap goes the pointer.

"Here is the IP . . ." pause to look at audience. "Initial Position for those of you who don't know. We hit the IP at thirty-eight. That gives your leader eighteen minutes to get straightened away. Questions?"

There are never any questions.

"Right. Our run-in time is seven minutes, we hit the reviewing stand at forty-five." Pause for effect. "That is the exact time of the 'general salute'."

The FPM is lost to the view of those half-way up the room. Enough oxygen remains to support combustion, however, and fresh cigarettes are lit. The non-smoker can now slide safely to the floor. He will not be missed.

"We have sixty-four aircraft, that gives us four spares. Do the spares know what they are to do?"

Four pilots relegated to be 'spares' nod affirmatively. They will get themselves airborne the same as everyone else and fit themselves into any slots that happen to go empty due to unserviceabilities. You can listen to all this from your place under the table.

"You section leaders can be prepared to step-down on the inside of the turns. Got that?"

There is sometimes more oxygen under the windows, if one is open. Crawl toward it.

"The sections flying line-astern will step-down to remain clear of jet wash."

The smoke is congregating at the window too? Crawl the other way, toward the door. There might be a crack under it. Feel your way among the legs.

"And watch your spacing . . ." the voice drones on.

Forget the voice. All you have to do is fly formation anyway. Lie flat. There, didn't I tell you? There is fresh air along the bottom edge of a door.

* * * * *

There is, indubitably, pleasurable excitement in flying fly-bys. Fighter pilots are inveterate show-offs no matter what they appear to be. So enjoy your brief moment on the stage. Taxi out with the mob, turn up your oxygen to avoid asphyxiation as everyone's tailpipe points directly at you. Things get better once you're airborne.

Tick-tick-tick goes the clock in the corner. What time did the Fly-Past Master say? No matter. You won't take-off until your turn. ROAR go the four J-47's of Alpha section. They take-off.

ROAR goes Bravo section, four Swords start rolling as Cocoa section edges out on the runway.

Your time! Delta leader is rolling out and where are you, faithful number Two? Too much throttle, too much . . . nose bobs as you save a wing tip by harsh use of brake. Thump thump thump, heart works okay. Reach down and turn off the oxygen. Line up in position

Tactical Flight Sabre 5's of No. 1 (Fighter) OTU, Chatham, New Brunswick, do a fly-by for radar scope watchers of near-by Ste. Margaret's Pinetree Line site. Though the denizens of Ste. Margaret's were within driving distance of Chatham, they still felt "bushed" in the New Brunswick woods.

beside the leader. He twirls his finger in the signal to wind up the rubber bands. ROAR goes J-47, and blends with the roar of the other three Sabres of Delta section.

Delta lead drops his hand and you release the brakes. Sabre stops shuddering and begins to roll. Leader creeps ahead. Whang! with the throttle. It was already at 100%. Slow down, slow down! Your mental pleadings have no effect on Delta leader's airplane. He's three feet ahead of you now.

His nosewheel begins to lengthen. Check back on the pole. Only two feet ahead, congratulations. Main wheels — tiny things for so big an airplane — blur and separate from the asphalt. Go flying. Left hand grabs at the gear handle, flies back to the throttle. Ease it off! Pour it back on as it starts its customary sink.

Leader's D-doors flump, the wheels begin their uncertain journey to the wells. The nosewheel D-door is the last to slam. Cleaned, it's a magic silver Sabre sliding over the greens and browns. Nudge in closer.

Bloody fine take-off, that. You wonder if anyone on the ground saw it.

A glance back beneath leader's tail. No sign of Three and Four. Return to that all-important wing tip. The leader's wing tip. You line up the tiny green nav light with his head. He hand signals the turn, and eases into it. And so do you. Tum-te-dum-dum. Some guys, you reflect, are just naturally good formation pilots.

Delta Three and Four close it up, and Delta leader closes with others. In no time it's a sky full of airplanes all going the same way. And now it's work. See-sawing on the throttle as Delta leader see-saws on his trying to formate on the formation leader who is intent only on making the IP on time. It can get wild.

But not today. The formation leader knows what he's about, Delta section is reasonably close to the head of the procession, and none of the turns have you eyeball to eyeball with Mr. Sun.

"Showcase formation," announces the leader, "we're

five seconds slow at the IP. Opening to eighty-nine."

You risk a glance at your rpm dial: 85%. No sweat.

Aside from the normal sweat, that is. Formation flying — when it's done for show — can be hard work. It's a matter of concentration. Other things too, of course. Anticipation of the leader's actions, of throttle lag and power surge, airplane characteristics. That sort of thing.

Hitch yourself sideways in the seat. There, neck feel better? Peering hard port for extended periods of time can get agonizing. What's that you say? Forgot to loosen the shoulder straps to start with, and now the automatic harness lock has locked? Hmmm.

Using your famous fighter pilot's 'split vision', you may notice the radio compass needle swing as Delta section crosses the IP. Time to clamp. To settle into position so well that witnesses on the ground will think you're welded there. Concentrate on the wing tip, your distance out so that it will match your opposite number, the Three man. Fifty yards beyond him, is another diamond four. You hope they are flying the correct spread — like yours.

Work, sweat, concentrate. Just a little while longer. Forget your neck muscles. Don't bash the throttle. Relax on the pole. There, it needs a jab of trim. Funny you didn't notice sooner. Leader bobs . . . or did you drop? Ease it up. Slot man is five feet below the leader's tailpipe. He doesn't appreciate wingmen dropping.

The button of an unknown runway appears beneath. A pang of fright stabs deep. The reviewing stand is somewhere close. Hold it, hold it now. Along with the neck ache comes a trickle of sweat into one eye. It stings and smarts and your eye is awash with tears. Hold it, fly it smooth.

Rectangular blobs of green appear ahead and beneath your leader's snout. The hangar line. Somewhere a fathead general is saluting. You wonder if the sweat is trickling down his flanks. Or of his neck is crikked to the breaking point.

The "Sabre Knights" aerobatic team of the 325th Fighter Squadron, Hamilton AFB, California. (Photo: North American Aviation)

The hangars and the ant-like crowds slide under. You're by. The pass is complete. Delta leader lifts his hands and languidly spreads them outwards. 'Relax', he is saying. Gratefully you slither out three feet. The slot-man sees both you and number Three slide out, so he drops back three feet. The diamond looks the same, but everyone is relaxing.

* * * * *

Everyone likes to tell of the hairiest fly-past they ever participated in, and those Sabre pilots who flew in NATO Europe during the nineteen-fifties can probably tell the most hirsute stories of all. In the early years of that decade the fiascoes were apt to be generated by weather. In the latter years, more often by senior and desk-bound pilots who thought it glorious to lead but had forgotten how.

"Fly-past, chaps."

The winter rains beat against the windows and dribbled in malencholy rivulets from our unhangared Sabres. We hadn't turned a wheel in a week.

"The minister of national defense is visiting Gros Tenquin this Friday. Every squadron in Air Division is putting up twelve Swords."

Nine squadrons times twelve Sabres each equals . . . equals. The flight commander helped out.

"One hundred and eight Sabres."

"In the same patch of sky?" Incredulous voice.

"Right. Two Wing flies over here, picks us up, we fly over to Four Wing and pick them up. Then we all fly back to Gros Tenquin for the fly-past."

"They going to have enough fuel for all that?" grumbled someone.

The plan called for the three Sabre squadrons of 2 Wing (Gros Tenquin) to take-off one behind the other, fly to 3 Wing (Zweibrucken) where our three squadrons would fall in behind them, continue to 4 Wing (Soelingen) where three more outfits would tag on . . . and then back to GT for the ceremonial fly-past. From that point each Wing was free to return to its own base.

The briefing was held the day before. Our station C Ops O explained it.

"With eight squadrons stacked back at two hundred foot intervals, it leaves the last squadron at four hundred feet. Question?"

"What are the weather limits, sir?"

"If we don't have two thousand feet, we don't go."

It seemed fair.

The next day the rain had stopped. Now it was fog. We sat in the flight room kitted, but not really expecting to go.

"What's the ceiling now?" someone asked.

"Two thousand. It's the viz. We only got three miles."

I do not, personally, believe that we'd have flown a fly-past in that kind of weather had it not been for the gung-ho attitude of the chaps at Gros Tenquin. They

The view from the slot. Ventral view of a Sabre 5 from the back seat of a T-33, RCAF Station Trenton, Ontario. White streak is canopy-imbedded antennae.

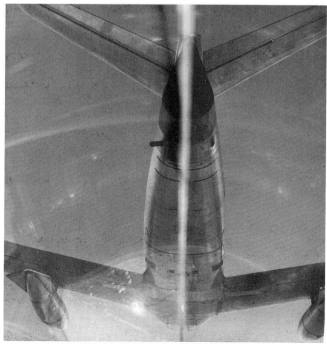

Tight diamond formation demonstrated by the "Minute Men" aerobatic team of the Colorado Air National Guard.
(Photo: North American Aviation)

may have been inspired by the presence of the minister of national defense, but I think not. The pilots of 2 Wing were just like that. If there was a chance that anyone else would chicken because of weather, they'd make it a point to go.

The schedule time to start engines came and went. We remained in the flight room waiting for the word to stand-down. Outside it had started to rain again. The phone rang and the flight commander answered. As anticipated, it was the C Ops O.

"They've left, sir? Right. Right. We go."

Twelve pilots won't fit in a doorway constructed for one. But it gave illustrious flight commander the chance to say:

"The GT guys are airborne. They'll be overhead in fifteen minutes."

That did not leave much time for the 36 Sabres of 3 Wing to fire-up, take-off and form-up. But we did. And the leader of the first 3 Wing squadron pulled smartly in behind the third 2 Wing squadron. Our particular squadron came next and hapless 413 Sqn brought up the rear. I say 'hapless' because of circumstance; the pilots of 413 that day brought nothing but honor upon themselves.

In the crush of getting airborne, no one paid too much attention to the rain, or the fog, or the indeterminate ceiling that was a mixture of both. The surprise awaited us up there. At a thousand feet the ground disappeared.

You might well ask how it was that the fifth squadron out of six fell into cloud when the preceding squadrons were supposed to be at successively higher altitudes. Well the 200-foot vertical displacement between squadrons had changed to 10-foot separation.

Eastward to 4 Wing.

Your correspondent was flying the box, which is as good a position as any for it permits you to observe what is going on all round. The claustrophobia induced by wing tips waving in your face is balanced by the blessing of not getting a crik in your neck. You avoid this by not moving in close to the leader's tailpipe until the final run-in. But I digress.

When we got to Soelingen, the home of 4 Fighter Wing, the ceiling had lowered to 800 feet. And lower than this over the hills of the Black Forest which lay just beyond. It was raining and the formations were in and out of cloud. In the gloom that lay beneath us, ghostly patches of stratus obscured the deeper gloom that was earth. It was a terrible day.

Apparently the 4 Wing types thought so too. The word filtered back: "Four Wing cancelled out."

Eminent good sense, I thought, but knew a perverse satisfaction too.

Ahead — quite out of sight — the formations were swinging westward for Gros Tenquin and the waiting minister of national defense.

"I can't see," someone complained.

"What's wrong?"

"Nothing. But if I fall out of this cloud, look out."

"Want to try it down here in the trees?"

For it was a fact that while the boys on the top of the turn were lost in clag, the ones fighting to hold the inside of the turn were dragging wing tips through the foliage.

As our squadron staggered round in this turn, I was alarmed by the proximity of the hills. Strips and tatters of ground fog clung to the wet pines and soggy undergrowth. My view was of the lead Sabre's tummy compressing an already thin horizon line. And I didn't know what 413 Sqn behind us was using for flying room.

We got away from the hills, recrossing the mud-roiled Rhein and on into France. Everyone breathed easier, even though the ceiling wasn't going up any. The rain was everywhere and I had opportunity to be glad that I was just one of the workers and not responsible for getting this gaggle to a fly-past, or home afterward.

Lower and steadily lower as the raggedy cloud pressed on the squadron ahead. It was — I hazard the guess — about 300 feet by the time the formation leader said:

"By the IP chaps . . . clamp."

Clamp? All right for him to tell his squadron to clamp, they were sitting fat at 300 feet. The rest of us had been flying 'clamped' for the past 15 minutes. It was 'clamp' or get scraped off. Clamp! Ha!

Ahead, in the rain-swept murk which I viewed beneath the oil-streaked aluminum slab that was my leader's belly, was 427 Sqn. We were following them. Trouble right now seemed to be that 427 Sqn were too low. I realized that they were just staying below who they were following, but we didn't have room to stay beneath them.

Tin hangars appearing out of the gloom. A wide grassy space that must be infield. Trees on the other side. A construction derrick at the level of my head. 413 Sqn behind us must, I thought, have broken off long before this. For we were at ground level.

Rain piddling down. Hangars coming on. Horizon gone above my glorious leader. Yowee! Small wet crowd standing on the concrete. An honor guard. Poor sods. What of the minister of defense? Still standing there? Surely not. But if he was, he was watching the hairiest fly-past he'd ever see.

Zap!

Somehow, and to this minute I don't know how, somehow I got over the hangar.

What about 413 Sqn? I winced and waited for the sound. Either the death shriek, or the announcement that someone had bought the ranchero. Nothing happened. We were sweeping over countryside once again. Wet brown fields lined by wet green trees. A church steeple stabbed upwards. What was happening to 413 Sqn? Had they gone home?

They were behind and beneath us. But they were pursuing a weaving course as entire sections of four flew between the hangars not over them, round the construction derricks, the trees and the church steeples that lined the escape route. For the affair wore the manner of a rout as we left Gros Tenquin for home.

Being short of fuel, and in suspect weather as it was, I suppose we should all have landed at Gros Tenquin. The thought never occurred. To our leaders — and indeed all of us — landing at GT would have been an admission of something or other. No one ever defined what.

But nobody thought of landing on the nearest jet runway, either. Heavens no. We all got back to Zweibrucken and gave the control tower operator the worst five minutes of his life.

The final four Sabres to land flamed-out on the runway.

Instructors from No. 1 (Fighter) OTU, Chatham, New Brunswick, fly close line-astern loop for photographer Barry Herron. Slot-man was F/L Ron Potter; leader unknown. Circa 1957.

Fighters Then and Now

Sopwith Triplane of #1 Squadron, Royal Naval Air Service, 1917. The Triplane won fame with "B" flight of Naval Squadron 10, destroying eighty-seven German airplanes during the summer of 1917. Armament was 1 Vickers machine gun; top speed: 117 m. p. h.

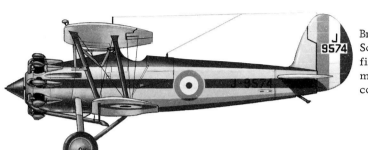

Bristol Bulldog IIA. The Bulldog entered service with #3 Squadron in 1929 and became one of the standard RAF fighters of the early and mid nineteen-thirties. An armament of 2 Vickers machine guns was carried. The ship could also be fitted with four 20 lb. bombs. Top speed was 174 m. p. h.

Lockheed P-38L of the 36th Fighter Squadron ("The Flying Fiends"), 8th Fighter Group, based on the island of Ie Shima during mid-1945. Pilot: 2nd Lt. Dino Cerutti. Armament: 1 20 mm. cannon, 4 .50 calibre machine guns, plus 2 500 lb., 1,000 lb., or 1,600 lb. bombs or ten 5 in. rockets. Top speed was 414 m. p. h.

Canadair Sabre 2 of the Yugoslav Air Force. Armament: 6 .50 calibre machine guns, 16 5 in. HVAR rockets, or 2,000 lb. maximum bomb load. Maximum speed: 679 m. p. h.

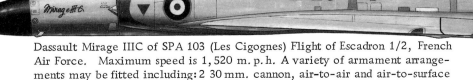

Dassault Mirage IIIC of SPA 103 (Les Cigognes) Flight of Escadron 1/2, French Air Force. Maximum speed is 1,520 m. p. h. A variety of armament arrangements may be fitted including: 2 30 mm. cannon, air-to-air and air-to-surface missiles, and various armament/fuel pods.

French Morocco

In those early days of NATO — most have forgotten this now — the French government had a policy of cooperation with its NATO allies. Yes, they did. And the French allowed the Canadian Sabre squadrons to use the airfield at Rabat, French Morocco, for air/air gunnery. There being an area over the Atlantic near-by for that purpose.

As it happened, our squadron was the first to visit the Moroccan site. Which is neither here nor there since it has nothing to do with the story. Suffice to explain that the African climate was excellent for our purposes. The days being sunny, if hot, and the visibility unrestricted.

The procedure followed by ourselves (and other squadrons, I believe) was to have one Sabre towing the flag and another three in the gunnery circuit. So that in any one day a pilot might normally expect to find himself airborne on three to four sorties, towing once perhaps, and shooting on the other three occasions. Which is more information extraneous to this tale.

It happened one day that by being first down to the flight line at 5 am, I managed to fly six trips before old Mr. Sun called a halt that day. A beautiful evening as I taxiied in for that last time and shut down. I was tired. Perhaps naturally, perhaps not. Due to the heat I'd given up wearing a G-suit in favor of T-shirt and stomach muscles. (You wrinkle them up.)

Imagine my surprise when Sam the Duty Pilot came loping across the tarmac waving and shouting at me.

"Hurry up!" In his hand was the flight authorization form. "You're going up again," he explained slewing to a halt.

"I am?"

"Take three-oh-two." He pointed at Sabre 302. "We're going for time."

It appeared that 434 Sqn was within striking distance of flying 100 hours in a single day. A record at that time.

"Go and fly," Sam instructed, looking with satisfaction at my initials which testified that I'd been briefed and knew exactly the duty to be performed. "Just fly."

"How long?"

"An hour at least."

Sabre 5 belonging to station flight RCAF Station Summerside, Prince Edward Island, 1955.

I groaned. The thought of sitting for another hour — my seventh trip of the day — didn't appeal.

"Fly." And Sam stalked away.

Well, as these things are often wont to go, the trip was pleasurable. The evening indigoes were upon the Moroccan landscape, it was cool, and there were no wingmen to worry about. At 3,000 feet I was into sunshine. Off to my left was the wrinkled Atlantic and a few miles out the dark ribbon of stratus normally to be found there. Beautiful evening.

And since it was such an evening, I decided to fly north to Gibraltar. To see that famous chunk of British Empire insurance. At 45,000 I finally levelled and continued north following the coastline to Tangier. That famous city was merely a cluster of lights in a darker blob set on a dark coast. But I knew it was Tangier.

Across that burnished strip of water known, prosaically, as the Strait of Gibraltar, lay Gibraltar. Bastion of British . . .

"All Sunfish aircraft, all Sunfish aircraft." It was Sam the duty pilot, on the radio. "Return to base. I say again, return to base."

It was a most unusual call, but the urgency in his voice was unmistakable. I was already bending it round toward the south as he explained to whoever was still flying.

"A cloud deck is moving in from the west."

At 45,000 feet in the sunshine, without a cloud in sight, it is sometimes difficult to get alarmed. But I was apprehensive as I acknowledged the order to return.

"Where are you now?" asked Sam.

"Gibraltar."

"Okay. I got a pair and two singles up north there somewhere. Keep your eye open for them."

I didn't want the bother of picking up anyone, so I said:

"They'll be home before me."

"I might not be able to raise them."

He meant on the VHF. The control tower at Rabat only had a few frequencies. After awhile, maybe ten minutes or so, Sam came back to tell me:

"I got two of them. They're doing a frequency search. They'll pick you up on the way in." Then he added, sort of as if to convince me. "They're junior pilots."

We had several new pilots on the squadron.

"Rog'," I answered. "What's your weather now?"

"It's okay at the moment," he still sounded worried, "but there's this low deck of stratus just to the west."

"How far?"

"Half mile. But it's moving."

Still in the sunshine at 45,000 feet, and still no cloud in sight below, it was easy to sound confident.

"How is the viz under it?"

"Looks okay."

My worries left me. What is a little bit of stratus?

So I thought about my other responsibilities.

"What altitude are these guys at?"

"Stand-by one." And in a little while he came back on. "They're at twenty-five."

"Okay. Tell them I'll pick them up at fifteen thousand over Port Lyautey."

Lyautey was just north of Rabat, along the coast, and its oil storage tanks and airstrip made it easy to see from the air.

"Okay," Sam agreed. "You can get them on tactical."

Tactical frequency. The one we used for gunnery. I switched channels, established contact. No sweat. Throttle back, boards out, descending. Still no clouds underneath. Still in the sunshine. Grand day. Beautiful. and a bit of excitement to finish it off. What could be better?

At 25,000 feet, far ahead of me, I saw the skinny layer of purple cloud. It was patchy. Pick a hole, any hole. Fuel? Mmm . . . fifteen minutes. Pas de sweat.

"Okay Red leader, got you in sight. We'll close up."

I had, magically, become Sunfish Red leader. Two silver Sabres attached themselves to my starboard wing. Grand. Sun going down over the Atlantic. Purple cloud layer shot through with holes ahead of us. Two more Sabres orbiting over one of the holes. I told them to join up on the left. Now I had a five-plane vic.

"Your position, Red?"

Sam there in the control tower was worried.

"It's okay," I reassured him. "Over Lyautey, still in the sunshine."

"It's dark here," grumbled Sam.

"Tell him to turn on the runway lights."

'Him' being the French tower operator.

"There are none."

I'd forgotten that. As we vacated 12,000 feet, the sun was a gold crescent on the horizon. The cloud ahead suddenly looked more solid. A pang of intelligent fright went through me. The radio compass didn't appear to be working.

"Is the beacon on?" I asked politely.

"They haven't got it on today. He says the man who can put it on is away to Casablanca on holidays."

That sounded like the French all right.

"Okay." And I turned back toward Port Lyautey where I'd seen that last hole. "I'll let down visual and take a homing."

The French had an ADF Homer at Rabat. A pre-WW II relic that was operated manually. Sam hammered that hope.

"It isn't working today."

One's cockpit cross-check can become pretty rapid. Fuel: 7-8 minutes. And that's about the only check that counts. As for getting home to Rabat, it was to be strictly 'pilot dead-reckoning'.

The hole in the stratus cloud was still waiting for us. Underneath was a shock. It was dark. Not really dark, but almost. The cloud was about 700 feet off the desert, and it seemed we were flying under water.

I snicked on the nav lights and my wingmen did the same. They looked pretty. As did the soft red glow of my instruments.

I looked morosely at the cheerful sprogs formating on me. They were mere silhouettes. Purple desert unrolled beneath us. How long would it take to fly from Lyautey to Rabat? I hadn't the faintest. And how was I going to see an airfield that didn't have any runway lights? That too, was an inscrutable mystery.

Five minutes fuel remaining. We should have been there. Outside, the world was asleep, even if the western horizon did still show grey light. Under this cloud it was night.

A night bale-out? Five of them? Or a formation forced-landing on the desert. As usual, the scene preceding the court martial came to mind: "You fool! You bungling fool'!

Well? What to do. Start a square-pattern search? Let these cheerful wingmen know that I don't know where I am? No, heck no. Never tell a wingman anything. It's the first law of the fighter pilot.

We flew on. Not into the gathering darkness, it had already gathered. Just on and on. For a minute, at least. Above us, a black oily roof of cloud. Below, the desert. To either side, the cheerful gleam of my wingers' nav lights. Two hundred pounds of fuel. Three minutes?

Old buddy Sam to the rescue.

"You're getting close, I can hear you."

"Well step outside and 'see' me."

"Okay!" said Sam. "I got you now. Turn twenty starboard and it'll bring you out over the runway."

There, sure enough, in the gloom and the dark, was the ghostly outline of a runway. Half a mile.

"Red, echelon starboard."

And I didn't watch them go across. I was too busy enjoying the sight of that runway. It was dark enough when we landed, to need landing lights to taxi in.

Sabre 5 over Cartierville Airport, Montreal, Quebec, site of Canadair Limited.

Air-to-air gunnery target, "the flag", was of nylon weave with aluminum thread for radar gunsight reflectivity. Flag was six feet wide, twenty feet long. Iron bar at front end was lethal to Sabres which flew into flag trying for a good score. Note rocket rails on Sabre 5 breaking away from the flag.

Flag Shooting

There is nothing marvelous about air/air gunnery with a Sabre. The airplane is, as they say, a stable gun platform. There are three .5 calibre machine guns on either side of the nose intake; and a radar gunsight to do the most difficult work for the pilot. That is, to figure out the range.

We flew three Sabres in the circuit at a time, each firing different colored ammo. Another Sabre towed the flag which was of nylon weave and had a radar reflector of dubious worth installed on the front. This angular alloy ball later gave way to aluminum foil woven into the nylon itself, a much more satisfactory arrangement.

At the time of which I speak, however, average gunnery scores in the Canadian squadron were something less than 20%. With the improved gunsights in the Sabre Fives and Sixes which succeeded our old Sabre Two's, gunnery scores went up to the plus 80% range.

The circuit itself was standard. The shooters flew parallel to the target, 1000 feet above and to the landward side. The short diving attack on the flag was meant, if I recollect rightly, to give you a 100-knot speed advantage on the target. The idea was to place the gunsight pipper on the bullseye of the flag, track it smoothly with a minimum of G-loading, and, providing

Gunnery flight line-up of Sabre 5's, No. 1 (Fighter) OTU, Chatham, New Brunswick. The armed fighters were parked tail toward the hangars. Gunnery aircraft, subject to continuous G loadings in the gunnery pattern, bent sooner than the others. In the trans-sonic range they either rolled, tucked or porpoised.

that the radar lock-on light was glowing in your face, you could squeeze the trigger when the little range drum on the gunsight suggested that now was the time.

Confusing? Well the basic idea was to put the little bullets through the big flag. Since the bullets had paint daubed on them, a smear of color was left on the nylon threads and the hit could thus be identified as someone else's.

Being coldly analytical about the whole business — and we fighter pilots are that — good gunnery is a simple function of smooth flying and careful concentration.

As the end of the second week hove into view, there was some discussion about my progress as a gunner among my groundcrew friends. "When are you going to hit it?" was perhaps the kindest of the many questions.

Well I was trying.

"We gave you green ammo," muttered one of the armourers in my ear just prior to one trip. "When we count 'em you'll get all the blues and purples too."

The groundcrew counted hits. And there was always arguments between the blues, greens and purples. But even at that, I didn't get a good score. The squadron gunnery officer called me to look at my camera gun films. After the whirring had ceased, and the light went on again, he was baffled.

"I don't know what's wrong. Your film looks average."

That made me feel better. All the way out to the airplane. There was a group of the groundcrew waiting for me.

"Listen, Chickenhouse," said the leader. "You're making us look bad. We go round saying what a great fighter pilot you are, and then you don't hit the flag."

I told them about the film.

"Never mind the film. Shoot holes in the flag instead." And then he added: "We checked and re-checked this gunsight. You got the best one in the squadron."

Touched by their solicitude, I went out and really concentrated. I really sweated those attacks out. Fantastic concentration. Superbly flown. I could see that flag rumpling with the sheer weight of lead going through it.

"How'd ja do?" said one of the group of sun-tanned kids waiting for me to climb out.

"Better. Much better," I admitted modestly.

It was a 9% score. The squadron low for the day. They left me standing in front of that remarkably virgin flag. Without speaking.

The final day of the shoot arrived. My groundcrew friends decided, apparently, to try once more for me. One of them said as I hove round the corner of the op's building: "Get 432, she's hot."

So I managed to wrangle Sabre 432. When I got out to it, a delegation was waiting. T-shirted kids and bare-backed kids. Armourers, radar tech's and others. Friends.

"You got the best airplane," said the spokesman. "We're giving you the best gunsight we've got."

"Purple ammo," said an armourer.

For scoring purposes. And the leader added:

"Four guns instead of two. You should double your score."

As I was strapping-in, one of them climbed up on the side and leaned into the cockpit. He loosened the film magazine on the gunsight. I was surprised.

"The little sprocket . . ." I started to say.

"You won't be bringing back any pictures," he agreed. "How about some hits this time."

This, obviously, was an ultimatum.

"Look," I said, launching into a much thought-out argument on the possibility of some fighter pilots just naturally not being marksmen.

"Get some hits." And he jumped down and walked away.

Where do good gunnery scores come from? They are a simple function of smooth co-ordinated flying, careful tracking of the target, and a gentle squeezing of the trigger. I'd tried all that jazz. There was only that other way left.

"Red Two in," I announced, "first pass."

Red leader was reversing down there below me. It was time to crank her off the perch and charge in for the sighting pass.

Little white flag getting bigger. G-meter steady at 4, dropping off to 3, then 2. Radar lock-on light glowing. White pipper on grey flag. Steady, steady. Shoot! I didn't shoot.

Big white flag getting bigger, bigger. Yowee! Shoosh, flag flashes by the canopy top.

Thump thump thump, heart flutter? Murmur? Thump thump thump. Why didn't you shoot? Scared? Pull you dull sod, pull. Back upon the perch. Reverse. Ah, there's the flag. Red One is reversing on his attack. Your turn.

"Two in." What a wonderful calm voice you have.

The big flag getting BIG. It fills the cockpit, the horizon, the world with its grey fluttering mass. Brr-rr-rrrt! BREAK! Zung. Below the critter.

This goes on for about twelve more passes. Like a kamikaze. I'm hurling myself at the foe. Foe being flag. Brrrrt! go all the guns. At the very last instant

they go like that. It's after the last instant that we break to avoid colliding with the target.

Never was the clunk of empty breach blocks a more welcome sound. I didn't have to make any more attacks. The rest of Red section was ready to go home too.

"Close it up, Red Two."

Close it up? I was flying ten feet from his wing tip. How dangerous can it get? Anyway, the strange formation got back to Rabat airfield and this shaking right hand managed a round-out at the appropriate time.

There was a worried-looking reception comittee waiting for me to shut down and climb out.

"Did you hit anything?"

"I dunno."

"Well why don't you get out?"

They were always bugging me.

Anyway, to make a glorious story more glorious, we counted the hits on the flag. It was a fantastic 28%, the day's high score.

"Too bad about that sprocket not being engaged," said the gunnery officer when he heard. "If you had brought back some film we could have seen what you were doing different."

Sabre 5 breaking away from the flag.

Sabre 2 "firing-in" at gun pit. Tracer was employed for purposes of photo; cockpit light turned on for same reason. Armourers usually fired-in .50 calibre machine guns in pairs. Adjustments were to concentrate the zone of fire at a predetermined distance ahead of the Sabre.

The Boys From The Stable

No. 1 Overseas Ferry Unit, RCAF, was formed in Oct. 1953 for the purpose of flying newer models of Sabres to Europe to re-equip the Canadian squadrons serving with NATO. In June 1957, when the last Sabre Six was delivered to Europe, and the last Sabre Five flown back to Canada, the OFU folded.

During its short lifetime, the OFU ferried more than 1000 Sabres and T-birds across the Aatlantic without the loss of a pilot. It set a safety record for thousands of jet hours flown accident-free. It set a trans-Atlantic ferry record, and a cross-Canada speed record.

On paper the OFU sounds good. And it was good. But it couldn't have seemed that good to Squadron Leader Bob Middlemiss who organized and ran the outfit through most of its existence.

When the call went out to the Sabre squadrons of Air Division to supply pilots to the new ferry unit, each squadron commander viewed it as a heaven-sent chance to rid his squadron of its bad one.

Thus the OFU was a repository. Here gathered the malcontents, the agitators, the lushes and the gladiators. The perpetrators of misdeeds and atrocities. The senior officer baiters, the pub dismantlers and the ne'er-do-wells. They came to the OFU complete with legend and reputation.

If you were a pilot with the OFU, it was assumed that: you were a bad-actor before you came; you were being ousted from the RCAF as soon as possible; you could be expected to cause more trouble before that happy date.

These assumptions were usually valid.

S/L Middlemiss, saddled with the oddest collection of drivers since Claire Chennault's AVG, had a stock speech for newcomers.

"I've read your records," he'd say, glaring at the bagged individual in front of his desk. ". . . and I know you're a louse-up artist." Pause. "Just don't try to louse up my outfit."

This was sheer bravado, but I must say that Middlemiss carried it off well.

So okay. What about the job. What did they do. They flew all these Sabres across the Atlantic via Greenland, Iceland and Scotland.

In sections of four, ten minutes apart, they took off from Montreal for Goose Bay, Labrador. The track followed the wide St. Lawrence as far as Seven Islands, then struck cross-country to the Goose. There were Americans at Goose Bay.

"You will, under no circumstance, tangle with the Yanks," admonished S/L Middlemiss. "If they bounce you, let them."

Which sounded all right in the briefing room. Most section leaders adopted a 'one cheek only' attitude. They wouldn't attack any F-89's, F-100's or humble T-33's belonging to the USAF, but if attacked themselves, would hassle for five minutes. Leaving enough time to land ahead of the following Random section.

Due to the absence of alternate airfields, and the uncertainties of Greenland weather, Random often stalled at the Goose for weeks. Finally however the shriek of Orendas along the line would announce their departure.

In the cockpit, excitement. Beneath and receding, was a lake splattered Labrador. Section leader straightening on Joe Hurley's heading.

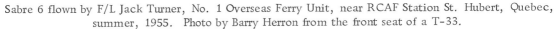

Sabre 6 flown by F/L Jack Turner, No. 1 Overseas Ferry Unit, near RCAF Station St. Hubert, Quebec, summer, 1955. Photo by Barry Herron from the front seat of a T-33.

Sabre 6 section led by F/L Jack Turner near St. Hubert, Quebec, summer, 1955. Other OTU pilots in ascending order: F/O Ken Young, F/O Len Pappas, F/O Ray Hodgins.

...route to NATO Europe, summer, 1955.
...200 U.S. gallons each.

at Narsarssuak were interesting. Groundcrew waiting to park us. The Americans think of everything.

"Okay, chaps," Random leader was apt to say at debriefing, "Weather looks good for tomorrow. We'll brief at five o'clock."

In the morning, he meant.

"What's doing at the Officers Club, sir?"

Reluctantly, almost reluctantly, S/L Middlemiss would admit:

"We've been invited to a Texas Nite."

A Texas Nite. Last time it was a Polynesian Nite. The time before that, a Las Vegas Nite. And a Seafood Nite, and a Rose Bowl Nite. They had Pirate Nites, Hoe-

Less than an hour later the snowy peaks of "Sunny Southern" Greenland were in sight. If the weather was CAVU, the section leaders started down well out to sea. By the time the four-plane hit Simiutak island at the mouth of the fjord, they were on the deck. Fifty miles, give or take, to Narsarssuak.

Ice pans on a black sea. A wrinkly black mirror flecked with white blobs that grow into ice floes and sometimes cathedral-size bergs. A grey weathered fishing smack, crew waving madly. Dip a wing at them. Island with a Danish fishing village clinging to the rocks.

Into the fjord. Stark brown walls, ancient rock stained with moss and seamed by rivulets. It's the same sight that greeted the first Viking longboat that arrived here 1,000 years before us. Not a weather radar to their name.

"Pulling up, Delta."

Almost there now, the Random sections climbed to circuit height for the pitch. The long runway huddled beside the saddleback looked good. One end of it lapped at the frigid waters of the fjord, the other end dropped into rocks.

"Delta on the pitch."

One second break, pick up the spacing on the downwind. Wheels, throttle, flaps on base leg. Approach now, make an S-turn to dodge a friendly iceberg. Landings

down Nites, and Dancing-Every-Saturday Nites. All very expensive, and all free. The Officers Club at Narsarssuak had to spend the profits from their slot machines.

"What's a Texas Nite?"

"Hamburgers?" asked a naive someone.

"Hamburgers! They've flown in a Texas longhorn. They'll barbeque the thing right in the Club."

Americans, in isolated places, are capable of feats that must confound their enemies even as it amazes their friends.

"I'd suggest you chaps get to bed . . ."

S/L Middlemiss was talking to the rumps of the Herd as they jammed and struggled in the doorway. It was Texas Nite in Greenland.

* * * * * *

Five in the morning in Greenland is like 5 am nowhere else in the world. It's cold and it's black and the eternal winds howl across the Ice Cap and venturi down the canyons.

The bus is at the barracks at quarter to.

"Where is everybody? Okay, we'll stop at the Club."

Flying Officer Verne Cottrell walks out to his Sabre 6 at Goose Bay, Labrador for the flight to Narsarssuak, Greenland. Packing Sabre cockpit with uniform, personal effects and flat hat took large amounts of ingenuity. (Random 17, 1955)

On any given night, there are always representatives of the Stable to say goodbye to our American hosts.

" 'Bye American hosts, see ya next time."

No reply, the last host having succumbed.

Briefing was at five, and it was the only sleep many of the boys got. They slumbered while the forecaster told tales of cols and ridges, millibars and dew points. It mattered nought, for if the decision was 'go' . . . a weather briefing was superfluous.

Grey dawn was unaffected by the Orenda thunder booming in the rock-walled fastness of the fjord as the Sabre sections bounded into the air, flattened as the gear folded, then swept out over the black water.

Keflavik, Iceland was next. Another American base, with more Americans in need of education, enlightenment, and that hearty Canadian good-neighbor treatment. They got it, too. By dint of a stupendous effort, a feat of collective will-power, the Stableboys always and somehow managed to out-last their hosts.

The situation was different at the next stop, RAF Kinloss, Scotland. The base was inhabited by Englishmen — occupation forces according to the villagers — who flew four-engine Shackletons on coastal patrol. Since the Brits here misread that hearty Canadian good-neighbor treatment for boorishness, there was never much hospitality extended.

This lack of hospitality induced a back-lash effect in the Stable. Most unfortunate. Not only was the dialog between RAF and RCAF strained, it was almost non-existent. Except once when we were called together for a speech by a Brit squadron leader.

"Someone," he said, pale with emotion, "has been stealing Her Majesty's coal."

One scuttle of coal per week per officer's room was the ration. It wasn't enough for a night.

"We've decided to lock the coal up," he went on. "But it's a dashed poor show when you can't trust officers and gentlemen. . ."

He did not continue. Nor did the depredations on the coal pile cease. The padlocked door merely necessitated a midnight over-the-rooftops coal lift. Every night. Rain, snow, sleet or fog.

The atmosphere was not friendly.

In recollection, it was epitomized by the contempt on the face of that tweedy and far-away Shackleton pilot as he watched the exuberant Canadians surrounding themselves with palisades of beer bottles, then drinking themselves to the edge. A disgusting practice.

Air Division was next. Four Canadian bases in NATO Europe, each equipped with Sabres and each the home of some of the Stable. Here the Herd was welcome. Here old friends awaited, squadron mates assembled and the earnest drinking began.

Celebration flowed into celebration. And no outrage was so despicable as to lie beyond forgiveness. Barracks were dismantled, bars were broken up and friends' cars wrecked. The hospitality was unmatched and inexhaustible.

A day or two later the Herd was to be found wending its lowing way toward the North Star transport plane which took them back to Montreal.

On Setting A Speed Record

The morning Ralph Annis burst into the Stable waving a red-headline newspaper, was memorable.

"Look at this!" he roared indignantly. "The Navy set a cross-Canada speed record."

Sure enough, a Canadian Navy T-bird had wallowed along in a jet stream from Vancouver to Halifax in six hours and 20 minutes. Including a fuel stop at Lakehead. That wasn't what angered Annis.

"Why don't they sail their boats?" he went on. "Leave the flying to us."

But they hadn't. And there it was. Canadian Navy jets cross-Canada speed record. 6 hours 20 minutes coast to coast. In — of all things — a T-beast.

"We can do better than that," Annis vowed.

But it was almost a rhetorical statement, for the T-33 had greater range than our Sword Sixes, and there was no mid-air refuellers to speed us along our way.

Lakehead is almost exactly half-way across Canada. But the lone civilian operated fuel bowser made refueling there unwelcome. Too much time lost.

Gimli, Manitoba, was an RCAF station where we could get fast turn-around on fuel, but it wasn't any half-way house either.

"It's a thousand miles Vancouver to Gimli," said Ralph emerging from the maps momentarily. "We got 1200 miles range so we're fat getting there."

"How far Gimli to Halifax, Ralph?"

The black eyebrows knitted.

"Fourteen hundred."

"We can't make it."

Ralph scowled out the window at the long line of Sabres. They were being readied for a Random the following week. The published range for a Sabre Six with big drops was 1200 miles.

"That's still air miles," Ralph mused. "With a wind . . ."

He turned to his computer and twirled it for a while. The eyebrows remained wrinkled when he finished.

"Nuts," he muttered, tossing computer aside.

"What's wrong?"

He didn't answer the question.

"I'll phone the Canadair test pilots. Maybe these things will do better than 1200 miles."

According to the Canadair test pilots, the 1200-mile figure was valid. Annis wasn't satisfied.

"They don't know!" he said, hanging up the horn. "They never flew one for range."

No one, to my knowledge, ever accused Ralph Annis of being easily convinced. A day or so later he stuck his nose in my office door:

"Want to go flying?"

As we hoofed it out to the birds he laconically explained:

"I thought we'd go to Gimli, refuel and see if we can make it to Halifax."

Stationed as we were at Montreal, the flight from there to Gimli was no sweat. But the 1400-mile jaunt from GM to Halifax might be.

At Gimli we talked to an old friend, Ken Lett, who was a senior officer type wheel at Gimli. Ralph had worked for him when Ken ran the instrument school in Air Division. Ken thought the entire scheme was great.

"If it turns out you can make it," he promised, "I'll arrange a quick turn-around for your try at the record."

That afternoon we flew the 1409 miles non-stop to Halifax. Annis had 8 gallons of fuel remaining, I had 5.

"A piece of cake, sir!" crowed Annis to our CO when we got back to Montreal. "We can do it easy."

All that remained was permission from the crusty old air commodore who owned us. Annis and I went to his headquarters to convince him.

The meeting was august. That is, the personages sitting in the AOC's paneled office were august. Annis and I were the most junior officers there.

"Explain how you propose to do this," said the AOC without smiling. I don't know that he ever smiled.

The one thing going for us that morning was the fact that none of the august senior body officer types there had any jet experience. Perhaps it was this fact that encouraged Ralph Annis to his finest performance ever. With computer in one hand, chalk in the other, he stood before the blackboard and outlined the whole operation.

"There it is, sir," he concluded. "A piece of cake."

"Mmm," conceded crusty old AOC. "Go through that fuel consumption bit again. The Gimli to Halifax leg."

So Ralph explained it all again, twirling his computer

Overseas Ferry Unit pilots who set present cross-Canada speed record, August 29, 1956. Left to right: the leader, F/L Ralph Annis, F/O Bruce Merklinger, F/O Bernie Mc-Comiskey, F/O Chick Childerhose.

Sabre 5 believed to belong to RCAF Central Experimental & Proving Establishment. Photo was taken from a photo reconnaissance Lancaster of 408 Squadron north of Ottawa. Note wing fences on "hard-edge Five".

and burbling pounds per hour and gallons to pounds, Mach numbers and cruise configurations.

"All right," interrupted the AOC, slapping his hand on his desk. "Everyone out of here. I want a word with you two alone." He was looking at Ralph and me.

He continued looking at us for some time after all his staff officers had left. Then he leaned forward in his chair, fists gently before him on the desk and said:

"All right you sods, I know you can't make it."

After a shrivelling silence he continued:

"But I'm going to let you try."

Ralph Annis found voice.

"Thank you, sir. I'm sure . . ."

"Just one thing," interrupted the AOC, "if you are obliged to do a silk letdown into the New Brunswick woods, I advise you to keep on walking."

He glared at us both and thumped his fist in measure with the words:

"Because I'll have the two of you nailed to that wall!"

* * * * * *

With this encouragement we returned to base to plan the assault on the record.

Four Sabres were planned, one pair to fly high and throttled back to try it non-stop Gimli to Halifax, the second pair to fly with everything-to-the-wall with a second stop at Montreal. We reasoned that one or the other pair would make a new record.

Two factors were essential: VFR landing conditions at Halifax for the first pair; and a following wind. Our unit CO threw in a joker.

"You'll only have three days to make your try. If you don't get away by then, bring the airplanes back home for Random."

We flew out to Vancouver on the Monday.

Tuesday the weather was bad at Halifax. Wednesday it was bad at Gimli. On Thursday — at black 5 o'clock in the morning — the man in the forecast office said:

"CAVU at Halifax today. Gimli is reasonably good, but Montreal . . ." he perused the hyroglyphics . . . "mmm. IFR all day."

It meant that Bruce Merklinger and Bernie Mc-Comiskey, who were flying the second pair balls-to-the-wall Gimli refuel Montreal and on to Halifax, would lose time making an instrument approach at Montreal.

"Can't be helped," Ralph said. "We go."

The mountains were bare outlines in a grewly dawn as we climbed into clammy flying suits.

"Give us thirty minutes, Merk," said Ralph in a final word of briefing to Bravo section. We'll see you in Halifax."

Strapping in. Ahead, the mountains are pink outlined. Two airplanes away Ralph Annis stirs the air with a finger. The start engines signal.

WHUMP. The big Orenda catches fire. Crescendo scream blocking out the world. All the little needles on all the little dials rise smoothly. Each with its message of reassurance.

Fast, let's make it fast. Pressures okay, temperatures check. Warning lights flicking out. Radios working. Flaps down, hydraulic systems check. Controls functioning. Ralph interrupts.

"Taxi clearance."

"Roger Brandy . . ."

Morning mist, ankle-deep and swirly, parts to let us by. Pointed east where black mountains rise. How will we get over those?

Throttle sliding up the wall. Sabres rolling, tiny wheels blurring underneath. Ralph's nosewheel lengthens, hangs like an elephant's trunk. Airborne. Flick with the wheels. Fuel heavy we sink, then surge ahead. The wheels slam into the wells.

"Brandy, you're off at fifty-eight. Good-luck, chaps."

"Roger tower." Ralph scours his brain for the appropriate something. "We'll see you."

To our left is Vancouver. A scatter of lights in haze-ridden darkness. Vancouver sleeps, unaware of our great adventure.

I laugh at the conceit. But the laugh is pleasure too, for it's our adventure. Ralph's and mine. And even if we don't manage a speed record it's a fine adventure. Go back to sleep all you prunes who will never fly a Sabre.

Sunlight at 10,000 feet. The mountains are immediately less forbidding. At 35,000 feet we own sole rights to interior British Columbia.

Who can own British Columbia? Sometimes at dawn or dusk when the earth remains in darkness and you are flying in pink sunlight, you own everything you can see.

"Brandy Alpha is by Kimberley, Calgary next."

Kimberley is a mining town in the eastern-most fringes of the Rockies.

"Call by Calgary," says the man from Kimberley.

Far beneath us the miniature grey crinkled mountains slide into the greens and browns of the foothill country. Scattered low cloud becomes a layer and our journey is now an exercise in navigation. The sweep hand marches round the clock, the only moving dial in the shop.

"By Calgary," says Ralph.

A man on the ground repeats it back, and again we are alone. Alberta recedes and we're into Saskatchewan. Bright sunlight beating into the cockpit. Check the dials, the radio ident's, our navigation. Cross-check our position.

"Broadview, Ralph."

He blips his mike button in acknowledgment. Ralph doesn't know I played ball at Broadview once. Had my hitting shoes on that day. Two doubles and a home-run. Only time I ever hit a home-run in my life. The center fielder stretched over the fence and caught it. The clod.

Into Manitoba. Gimli air base is somewhere ahead of us. Unbroken layer of cloud hides the earth. Too bad, the three big lakes of central Manitoba make visual navigating easy. Are they waiting for us at Gimli? Fuel bowsers and start carts. Get in and get out. That's what we wanted to do. Gimli tower called us long before we expected it.

"Brandy Alpha, you're cleared for a straight-in approach. Traffic has been cleared."

Someone down there likes us.

Sixty miles out we nose over and start down. The hiss of pressurization is all that's left of noise as we ride the Mach needle down and down. Into the dripping grey blankness of cloud, and out again.

Green world beneath. 550 knots indicated and the white sheets of compressibility shock waves dance over Ralph's Sabre. Thirty miles to slow down in.

"Dive brakes, Alpha."

The doors wedge into that battering airstream. The speed falls back, the shock waves disappear. Ralph calls the tower.

"Ten miles, initial and landing clearance."

"All the way, Alpha. Check the gear."

Wheels thud into position, flaps grind down. We make it a formation landing.

At the far end of the runway are the waiting fuel tenders. As we spin the Sabres round and cut the engines, ground crews swarm over us. The JP-4 is gurgling into the tanks before the turbines quit their moan.

Sabre 5 of 411 (Fighter) Squadron Auxiliary, over Niagara Falls. Photo by Barry Herron from front seat of T-Bird flown by F/L Jim Lumsden. Sabre pilot, F/O Chick Childerhose. Tourists and honeymooners were treated to spectacle of T-33 chasing a Sabre into the mists of Horseshoe Falls as Herron kept saying, "You gotta get lower!"

The author and F/L Ralph Annis, a few minutes after landing at Halifax, Nova Scotia, August 29, 1956.

"How's the oxygen, sir?" says a voice in one ear.

"Here's the weather to Halifax," says Ken Lett in the other. "You have a tailwind component Quebec to St. John."

"Wind them!" roars Ralph Annis as the refuellers scamper for safety trailing hoses and trucks.

Once again we're belting down a long runway. Nine minutes from wheels on to wheels off again. We carve eastward over Lake Winnipeg.

Radar picks us up in the climb.

"Alpha, this is Crabtree. Kenora is seventy nautical."

Kenora is in Ontario. Our route lies across scenic northern Ontario. A fine place to get lost.

In succession we cross Kenora, Pagwa and Kapuskasing. Then we're on the longest leg of the flight, 500 miles of unbroken wilderness to Quebec City. Quebec is where Ralph has to make his decision to try for Halifax, or divert back to Montreal for fuel.

But if we go back to Montreal for fuel, Bruce and Bernie would be certain to beat us. And if the weather had been good at Montreal, they undoubtedly would have. As things stood, Annis and I were just pottering along at altitude trying to save fuel by flying at modest throttle settings.

At Quebec City Ralph had to make the decision. It was apparent before we got there that we didn't have enough fuel to make Halifax.

"Brandy," said an unfamiliar voice over the air. "This is Flat-top One. I'm flying in a T-bird." It was the Air Commodore, bless him. "How is your fuel?"

"Halifax green," Ralph said. We were going on.

"Good." The air commodore seemed pleased.

Now the tension creeps into the cockpit. Check the

fuel, our position, the clock. Check the dials and cross-check the radio compass. What state oxygen? Fuel consumption? Try for the latest Halifax weather. It looks like we'll over-fly the weather system beneath us.

Across Maine and into New Brunswick. Still over cloud. Still checking. An endless round of the cockpit. There's Fredericton, a glimpse of runway through the cloud. We've over-flown the bad weather.

Old fuel gauge isn't looking good. St. John slides underneath. Another runway behind us.

"Fuel state, Chick?"

"I'm fat."

I think maybe we're trying to cheer each other up.

The Bay of Fundy, a black wrinkled mirror far below, appears through the cloud. Halifax Centre clears us to descend. Everyone working for us.

Throttles back to 'idle', save the fumes for landing. Cloud cover disappears ahead of us. Down down we go and the white mists of compressibility flicker round the canopies. Fuel gauge doesn't quiver any more.

25,000 feet, altimeter looping round the dial. 20,000 feet. Beautiful ancient Nova Scotia below. They grow apples in Annapolis Valley. Clock ticking toward the 58-minutes mark. Five hours even since we left Vancouver.

"Alpha, dive brakes go."

Sabre bucks and shudders. Slowing down. Somewhere up ahead Ralph must have the runway. Right now I just fly close formation. Ralph pulls the imaginary chain and an instant later his wheels fall into place.

Rows of trees flash by. Colored approach lights on a forest of barber poles. A puff of smoke as Ralph's wheels touch the asphalt. Bump. We're on and rolling with him.

"Alpha, you're down at fifty-eight minutes, thirty seconds past the hour."

We'd made it in just over five hours.

Bruce Merklinger and Bernie McComiskey arrived a few minutes later. They'd done it in 5 hours 12 minutes. Given good weather at Montreal, they'd have beaten our time quite easily.

* * * * * *

On the following pages sections of the F-86E Flight Handbook are presented. Certain performance charts and technical data have been omitted in the interests of space.

EO 05-5E-1A

ROYAL CANADIAN AIR FORCE

AIRCRAFT OPERATING INSTRUCTIONS
SABRE 6

(This EO replaces EO 05-5E-1A dated 21 Feb 58 and all Revisions issued thereto)

ISSUED ON AUTHORITY OF THE CHIEF OF THE AIR STAFF

20 JUL 62

5E1A-01-1A

Sabre Aircraft

DESCRIPTION

INTRODUCTION

GENERAL

The Sabre 6 aircraft is a single-seat, -propelled monoplane, characterized by a tted, swept-back wing and empennage. De-ned primarily as a high-speed, high-altitude ter, the aircraft may also be used to attack und or naval objectives with gunfire, bombs, micals or rockets. The pilot is protected e and aft by armour-plate bulkheads. For general arrangement of the aircraft, see ure 1-1. For interior cockpit arrangements, e Figures 1-2, 1-3 and 1-4.

The power plant is an Orenda 14 axial-w, turbo-jet engine, providing approximately 75 pounds static thrust at sea level. An ctric starter-generator unit is provided for rting on an external source of power.

LEADING PARTICULARS

DIMENSIONS

The overall dimensions of the aircraft e as follows:

)   Wing Span   37.1 feet

)   Length   37.5 feet

)   Height   14.7 feet

WEIGHT

Approximate weights are as follows: Refer to EO 05-5E-8 for actual weights).

a)   Basic weight, (no fuel, oil, ammunition r pilot): 10,850 pounds.

)   Clean aircraft loaded, (including inter-al fuel, oil, ammunition and pilot): 14,370 ounds.

c)   With two 100 Imperial gallon drop tanks, ncluding full fuel, oil, ammunition and pilot): 6,135 pounds.

NOTE

1 Imperial gal. = 1.2 US gal.

(d)   With two 167 Imperial gallon drop tanks, (including full fuel, oil, ammunition and pilot): 17,315 pounds.

GROSS LANDING WEIGHT

5   The maximum gross landing weight for the Sabre 6 is 13,280 pounds. The approximate amount of fuel remaining at maximum gross landing weight with full weight of ammunition and oil is as follows:

(a)   Clean aircraft - 1700 pounds of fuel.

(b)   100 gallon drop tanks installed - 1500 pounds of fuel.

(c)   167 gallon drop tanks installed - 1350 pounds of fuel.

FUEL CELL AND OIL TANK CAPACITIES

6   Capacities are as follows:

(a)   Total available internal fuel is 357 Imperial gallons.

(b)   Total fuel with 100 Imperial gallon drop tanks installed is 557 Imperial gallons.

(c)   Total fuel with 167 Imperial gallon drop tanks installed is 691 Imperial gallons.

(d)   The maximum oil tank capacity is approximately 2.9 Imperial gallons with an expansion space of approximately 0.8 Imperial gallon.

FUEL SYSTEM

GENERAL

7   Five self-sealing fuel cells are installed in the aircraft; two in the fuselage, one in the centre wing section and one in each outer wing panel. Fuel is supplied to the engine from the centre wing cell which is gravity fed from all other internal cells except the aft

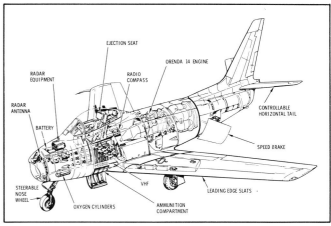

Figure 1-1 General Arrangement

fuselage cell. When 22 to 26 Imperial gallons of fuel have been used from the forward fuse-lage cell, the transmitter switch in the forward fuselage cell operates to start the transfer pump, transferring fuel from the aft fuselage cell via the centre wing cell. When 15 to 19 Imperial gallons have been transferred from the aft fuselage cell, the transmitter switch stops the transfer pump. When the forward fuselage cell has been emptied and 45 to 49 Imperial gallons remain in the centre wing cell, the transfer pump is switched off by the transmitter switch in the centre wing cell. The main fuel supply can be augmented by installing a 100 or 167 Imperial gallon drop tank under each outer wing panel. When neces-sary, the drop tanks may be jettisoned, Fuel from the drop tanks is forced, by compressed air from the engine compressor section, to the forward cell through a fuel level control valve, when the fuel level in the fuselage cell has fallen by 4 Imperial gallons. For a schematic diagram of the engine fuel system, see Figure 1-19.

8   There are individual filler points for each tank except the centre wing tank which is filled through the forward fuselage tank. The fuel

filler access doors cannot be closed unless the fuel tank filler caps are in the locked position. When refuelling the aircraft, the forward fuse-lage cell must be filled first in order to utilize the full capacity of the fuel system. If the wing tanks or the aft fuselage tank are filled first, fuel from these tanks will drain into the centre wing tank while the forward fuselage tank is being serviced. For servicing diagram, see Figure 1-5.

FUEL SPECIFICATIONS

9   For fuel specifications see Figure 1-6.

FUEL QUANTITY GAUGE

10   A fuel quantity gauge, located on the instrument panel, indicates total internal fuel in pounds. No gauge is provided for the drop tanks, but two lights on the instrument panel show when the drop tanks are empty. During take-off, with drop tanks full, the fuel quantity gauge will normally indicate a decrease until fuel begins to transfer from the drop tanks. At full power, fuel may be used at a greater rate than it is being transferred from the drop tanks.

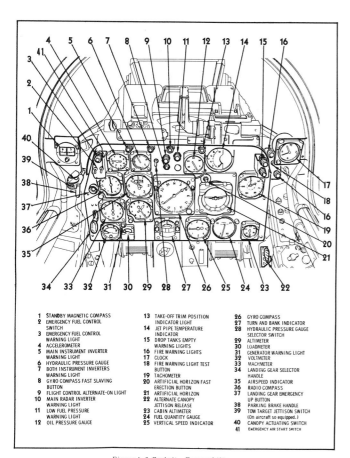

Figure 1-2 Cockpit - Forward View

1 STANDBY MAGNETIC COMPASS	13 TAKE-OFF TRIM POSITION INDICATOR LIGHT	26 GYRO COMPASS
2 EMERGENCY FUEL CONTROL SWITCH	14 JET PIPE TEMPERATURE INDICATOR	27 TURN AND BANK INDICATOR
3 EMERGENCY FUEL CONTROL WARNING LIGHT	15 DROP TANKS EMPTY WARNING LIGHTS	28 HYDRAULIC PRESSURE GAUGE SELECTOR SWITCH
4 ACCELEROMETER	16 FIRE WARNING LIGHTS	29 ALTIMETER
5 MAIN INSTRUMENT INVERTER WARNING LIGHT	17 CLOCK	30 LOADMETER
6 HYDRAULIC PRESSURE GAUGE	18 FIRE WARNING LIGHT TEST BUTTON	31 GENERATOR WARNING LIGHT
7 BOTH INSTRUMENT INVERTERS WARNING LIGHT	19 TACHOMETER	32 VOLTMETER
8 GYRO COMPASS FAST SLAVING BUTTON	20 ARTIFICIAL HORIZON FAST ERECTION BUTTON	33 MACHMETER
9 FLIGHT CONTROL ALTERNATE-ON LIGHT	21 ARTIFICIAL HORIZON	34 LANDING GEAR SELECTOR HANDLE
10 MAIN RADAR INVERTER WARNING LIGHT	22 ALTERNATE CANOPY JETTISON RELEASE	35 AIRSPEED INDICATOR
11 LOW FUEL PRESSURE WARNING LIGHT	23 CABIN ALTIMETER	36 RADIO COMPASS
12 OIL PRESSURE GAUGE	24 FUEL QUANTITY GAUGE	37 LANDING GEAR EMERGENCY UP BUTTON
	25 VERTICAL SPEED INDICATOR	38 PARKING BRAKE HANDLE
		39 TOW TARGET JETTISON SWITCH (On aircraft so equipped.)
		40 CANOPY ACTUATING SWITCH
		41 EMERGENCY AIR START SWITCH

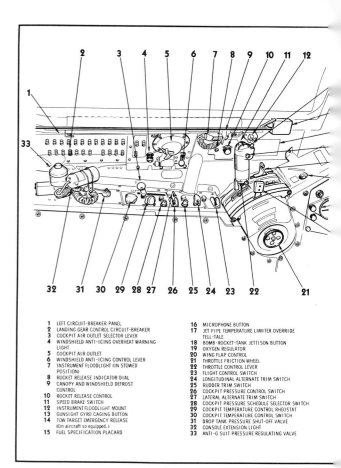

Figure 1-3 Cockpit - Left Side

1 LEFT CIRCUIT-BREAKER PANEL		16 MICROPHONE BUTTON
2 LANDING GEAR CONTROL CIRCUIT-BREAKER		17 JET PIPE TEMPERATURE LIMITER OVERRIDE TELL-TALE
3 COCKPIT AIR OUTLET SELECTOR LEVER		18 BOMB-ROCKET-TANK JETTISON BUTTON
4 WINDSHIELD ANTI-ICING OVERHEAT WARNING LIGHT		19 OXYGEN REGULATOR
5 COCKPIT AIR OUTLET		20 WING FLAP CONTROL
6 WINDSHIELD ANTI-ICING CONTROL LEVER		21 THROTTLE FRICTION WHEEL
7 INSTRUMENT FLOODLIGHT (IN STOWED POSITION)		22 THROTTLE CONTROL LEVER
8 ROCKET RELEASE INDICATOR DIAL		23 FLIGHT CONTROL SWITCH
9 CANOPY AND WINDSHIELD DEFROST CONTROL		24 LONGITUDINAL ALTERNATE TRIM SWITCH
10 ROCKET RELEASE CONTROL		25 RUDDER TRIM SWITCH
11 SPEED BRAKE SWITCH		26 COCKPIT PRESSURE CONTROL SWITCH
12 INSTRUMENT FLOODLIGHT MOUNT		27 LATERAL ALTERNATE TRIM SWITCH
13 GUNSIGHT GYRO CAGING BUTTON		28 COCKPIT PRESSURE SCHEDULE SELECTOR SWITCH
14 TOW TARGET EMERGENCY RELEASE (On aircraft so equipped.)		29 COCKPIT TEMPERATURE CONTROL SWITCH
15 FUEL SPECIFICATION PLACARD		30 COCKPIT TEMPERATURE CONTROL RHEOSTAT
		31 DROP TANK PRESSURE SHUT-OFF VALVE
		32 CONSOLE EXTENSION LIGHT
		33 ANTI-G SUIT PRESSURE REGULATING VALVE

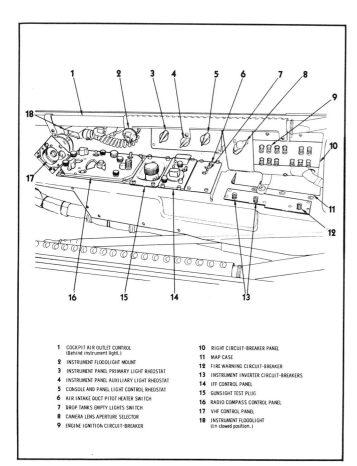

Figure 1-4 Cockpit - Right Side

1 COCKPIT AIR OUTLET CONTROL (Behind instrument light.)	10 RIGHT CIRCUIT-BREAKER PANEL
2 INSTRUMENT FLOODLIGHT MOUNT	11 MAP CASE
3 INSTRUMENT PANEL PRIMARY LIGHT RHEOSTAT	12 FIRE WARNING CIRCUIT-BREAKER
4 INSTRUMENT PANEL AUXILIARY LIGHT RHEOSTAT	13 INSTRUMENT INVERTER CIRCUIT-BREAKERS
5 CONSOLE AND PANEL LIGHT CONTROL RHEOSTAT	14 IFF CONTROL PANEL
6 AIR INTAKE DUCT PITOT HEATER SWITCH	15 GUNSIGHT TEST PLUG
7 DROP TANKS EMPTY LIGHTS SWITCH	16 RADIO COMPASS CONTROL PANEL
8 CAMERA LENS APERTURE SELECTOR	17 VHF CONTROL PANEL
9 ENGINE IGNITION CIRCUIT-BREAKER	18 INSTRUMENT FLOODLIGHT (In stowed position.)

<u>NOTE</u>

Because of the characteristics of the fuel system, the low pressure warning light may illuminate even though the aircraft has a full fuel load. However when the fuel remaining is 500 lbs. or less, illumination of this light may be accompanied by a flameout. Flameouts are most likely to occur under conditions of full throttle and high speed while manoeuvring at low altitude. However, flameouts could conceivably occur under any condition of flight if the fuel quantity is allowed to drop below 400 lbs.

11　A liquidensitometer system is installed. This system incorporates a guarded selector switch on the right forward console. When the guard is down, the switch is at the IN or normal position and the fuel quantity gauge will show the total fuel supply in pounds, corrected for any variation in fuel density. When the guard is raised and the switch moved to OUT, the system is adjusted to permit uncompensated gauge readings. This condition is used when a standard indication of quantity, such as a full condition after refuelling, is desired.

BOOSTER PUMPS

12　Two fuel booster pumps in the centre wing cell supply fuel, under pressure, to the engine fuel system. The pumps are actuated by initial outboard movement of the throttle control lever.

13　The booster pumps and the transfer pump in the aft fuselage cell may be tested on the ground by means of three switches, two in the left wheel well and one in the right wheel well. In order to test the forward booster pump, power must be supplied to the secondary bus.

SHUT-OFF VALVE

14　The fuel shut-off valve, located upstream of the filter, is controlled through the engine master switch.

DROP TANK PRESSURE SHUT-OFF VALVE

15　A drop tank pressure shut-off valve is located on the left aft console. When the valve is turned ON, both tanks are pressured by air from the engine compressor section. The pressure shut-off valve should be ON at all

times when drop tanks are carried to ensu that all fuel in the tanks is used to preve collapse of the tanks during rapid descent. T amber lights, one for each tank, indicate wh the tanks are empty. The lights are controll by a switch on the right aft console and shou not be switched OFF until both tanks are empt

OIL SYSTEM

GENERAL

16　Lubrication is provided by a pressure type oil system with a scavenge pump return the oil tank located at the forward right si of the engine. No manual control of the syste is provided.

OIL SPECIFICATION

17　The oil specification is 3-GP-901 (MIL O-6081, Grade 1010) and 3-GP-900 (MIL-C 6081, Grade 1005, winter) (latest issues). an emergency, OM71 3-GP-54 J D Eng R 2479/1 may be used, or provided temperature are not below -12. 2°C(10°F), 3-GP-38 (Utility Oil 44D) - classed as hydraulic fluid. If a emergency oil is used, an entry should be mad in the L14T, and the system flushed and re filled with the approved oil as soon as possible

OIL PRESSURE GAUGE

18　An electrical oil pressure gauge i located on the instrument panel.

HYDRAULIC SYSTEMS

GENERAL

19　The aircraft is equipped with three sep arate hydraulic systems; a utility system, a normal flight control system, and an alternate flight control system, see Figures 1-20 and 1-21. The systems are of the closed-centre constant-pressure type. The normal and alter nate flight control hydraulic systems supply hydraulic power for operation of the ailerons and the horizontal tail.

UTILITY HYDRAULIC SYSTEM

20　The utility hydraulic system is a constant-pressure type system powered by an engine-driven pump. The system supplies power for the operation of landing gear, speed

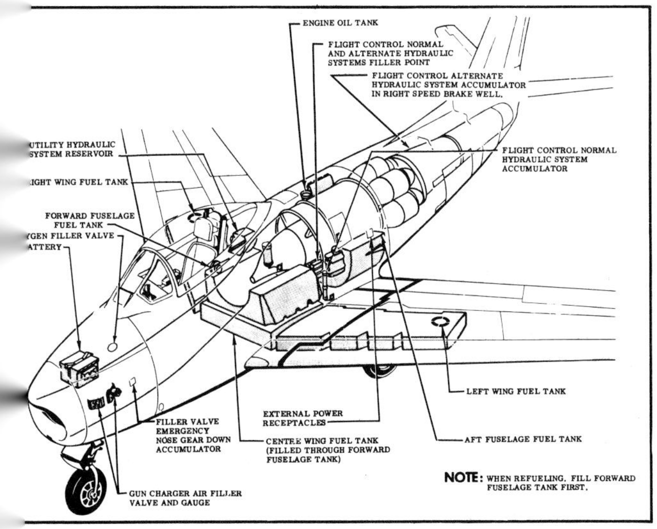

Figure 1-5 Servicing Diagram

akes, nose wheel steering and the wheel ake boost. While the operation of speed akes on a constant-pressure type system akes it unnecessary to return the control to utral after each operation, the neutral posin should be used. This will isolate the dividual systems from the pressure supply d prevent loss of fluid in case of a damaged ie.

STEM COMPENSATORS

Two spring-loaded compensators rece pressure surges, pressurize the return nes of the systems and maintain head presre on the reservoirs. Compensator pins, hich should be visible to indicate correct stem setting, may be checked through cess doors just aft of each speed brake.

EMERGENCY NOSE WHEEL LOWERING SYSTEM

22 The system consists of a hydraulic accumulator only. This provides sufficient pressure to lower the nose gear if the utility hydraulic system fails. The accumulator is automatically charged by utility system pressure.

HYDRAULIC PRESSURE GAUGE AND PRESSURE GAUGE SELECTOR SWITCH

23 A three-position toggle switch, marked UTILITY, NORMAL (flight control) and ALTERNATE (flight control), selects pressure gauge readings for the corresponding systems. For ordinary flight conditions the switch should be kept at NORMAL. Both switch and gauge are located on the instrument panel.

SURFACE CONTROLS

CONTROL COLUMN

40 The control column is of the normal stick type with a stick grip, see Figure 1-8 which mounts the following controls: radar target selector button, lateral and longitudinal normal trim switch, bomb-rocket release switch, nose wheel steering switch and the gun trigger.

41 To reduce stick forces in flight, the ailerons and horizontal tail-plane are operated by the surface control hydraulic power system. The control column actuates hydraulic valves through rod and cable linkage. The valves control the flow of fluid to hydraulic jacks which operate the ailerons and horizontal tail. Should the normal flight control hydraulic system fail, the alternate system will automatically engage. (Refer to paras. 23 through 27, preceding). Since the operating struts are irreversible, control surface attitude cannot change except in response to control column movement. In the event of a failure in the linkage between the control column and the artificial feel bungee, the horizontal stabilizer can be controlled through approximately half its maximum range by the use of trim. The rudder is cable operated and is provided with an electrically-actuated trim tab.

ARTIFICIAL FEEL SYSTEM

42 Because no feel of air loads can be transmitted through the irreversible hydraulic control system, an artificial feel system is installed. Normal stick forces resulting from G loads are provided through a bob-weight. Control surface air loads are simulated by bungees connected into the control system. The bungees apply loads in proportion to degree of control column deflection from neutral position. To trim the aircraft, the neutral position is changed by means of the normal or alternate trim switch, and bungees are repositioned correspondingly to maintain proper feel.

NOTE

In case of failure of the artificial feel system, while the stick forces are reduced to practically nil, the aircraft is still completely controllable. Care is required to avoid over-control.

RUDDER PEDALS

43 Pedal adjustment is conventional and exact alignment is facilitated by a position indicating wheel on the outboard side of each pedal. When the visible dial numbers correspond, the pedals are adjusted evenly.

CONTROLLABLE HORIZONTAL TAIL

44 The elevators and horizontal stabilizer are controlled and operated as one unit, known as the controllable horizontal tail. The horizontal stabilizer part of this unit is pivoted at the aft edge so that the leading edge can be moved up or down by control column action. The elevators are operated at the same time through mechanical linkage to the stabilizer section and move in proportion to movement of the stabilizer. Elevator travel is greater than that of the stabilizer. The controllable horizontal tail can be trimmed through use of either the normal or the alternate trim switch.

NORMAL TRIM SWITCH

45 Normal trim of the horizontal tail or of the ailerons is provided through a five-position knurled switch on top of the stick grip. This switch is spring-loaded to centre OFF position. When the lateral alternate trim switch is at NORMAL and the longitudinal alternate trim switch is at NORMAL GRIP CONT, lateral movement of the normal trim switch produces corresponding aileron trim. When the longitudinal alternate trim switch is at NORMAL GRIP CONT, fore-and-aft movement of the normal trim switch produces corresponding elevator trim. When the switch is released, it automatically returns to off and trim action stops.

LONGITUDINAL ALTERNATE TRIM SWITCH

46 A four-position switch on the left side of the cockpit provides an alternate trim circuit for the horizontal tail. Operation of this switch accomplishes longitudinal trim at the same speed obtained through use of the normal trim control. The switch is usually kept at NORMAL GRIP CONT, which allows the normal trim switch to be used. Holding the longitudinal alternate trim switch at NOSE UP or NOSE DOWN disconnects the normal trim circuit for the stabilizer, and trims the aircraft accordingly through the alternate trim system. The

itch is spring-loaded to OFF and is guarded the NORMAL GRIP CONT position. When e switch is at OFF, both the normal longidinal trim circuit and the alternate longitudal trim are inoperative.

ATERAL ALTERNATE TRIM SWITCH

A four-position switch on the left aft nsole provides an alternate means of lateral im. This switch is usually kept at NORMAL. olding the switch to either LEFT or RIGHT oduces corresponding aileron trim and disnnects the normal aileron trim circuit. The witch is spring-loaded to OFF. Both the ormal and alternate lateral trim circuits are operative when the alternate lateral trim witch is off.

UDDER TRIM SWITCH

8 An electrically-actuated rudder trim witch is located on the left aft console. The witch is held to LEFT or RIGHT for corresonding rudder trim.

AKE-OFF TRIM POSITION INDICATOR IGHT

9 An amber light on the instrument panel ndicates take-off trim position for ailerons, orizontal tail and rudder. The light will lluminate whenever any one of these controls s trimmed to the take-off position and will go out when the trim switch is released. It will lluminate again when the next control is rimmed for take-off.

NOTE

The take-off trim position indicator light does not operate when the longitudinal and lateral alternate trim switches are used.

50 The horizontal tail trim should be slightly forward of the fully aft position for take-off. Soon after becoming airborne, continuous forward trim will be desirable while accelerating to best climbing speed. Regardless of the trim position, a pilot of average strength will be able to overcome any stick forces encountered.

WING SLATS

51 Wing slats extend along the leading edge of each wing. Aerodynamic forces cause the slats to open and close automatically under varying flight conditions. At low airspeeds, (below 185 knots IAS with a clean aircraft), the slats open to improve lateral stability and reduce the stalling speed. In accelerated flight the slats open at speeds up to Mach 0.9, the actual speed at opening depending on the altitude and amount of G loading.

WING FLAPS

52 Slotted-type flaps extend from the aileron to the fuselage on each wing panel. Each flap is actuated through an individual electric motor and electric circuit. The flaps are mechanically interconnected to prevent either complete failure on one side or asymmetric operation. The flaps are loaded by the actuators in the up position to prevent airloads from moving them out of this position. No emergency system is provided, as there is sufficient protection present in the normal system.

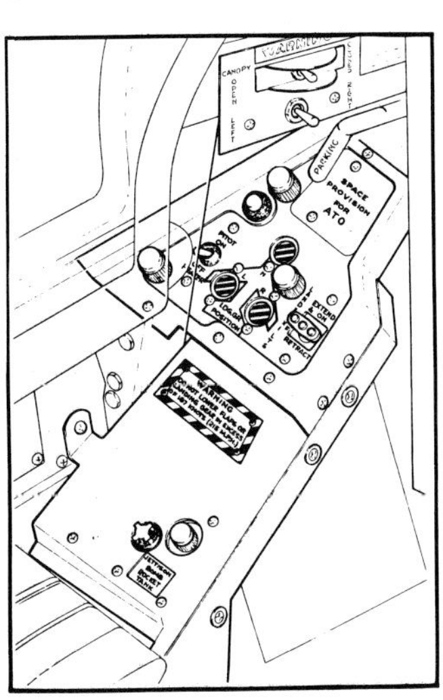

Figure 1-10 Left Forward Console

NOTE

If flaps are positioned only 1-1/2" down, they will not retract unless further down selection is made first.

WING FLAP CONTROL LEVER

53 The wing flap control lever, inboard of the throttle on the left console, moves in a quadrant marked UP, HOLD and DOWN. To move the flaps, the lever is placed at UP or DOWN and then returned to HOLD when the desired flap position has been obtained. There is no flap position indicator. A red line painted on the leading edge of the flap indicates flap take-off position when it becomes visible.

RUDDER CONTROL LOCK

54 A rudder control lock is permanently installed beneath the centre of the instrument panel. When the handle is pulled aft, a rudder cable lock is set to engage when the rudder is neutral. The nose wheel steering cable is locked at the same time. The other surfaces, being hydraulically operated, are irreversible and do not require a lock.

SPEED BRAKES

55 Hydraulically-operated speed brakes are located on each side of the rear fuselage.

SPEED BRAKE SWITCH

56 A switch on top of the throttle lever controls the speed brake hydraulic control valve. The switch has three fixed positions: IN, OUT and a neutral position which is indicated by a white mark on the switch guide. After the brakes have been opened or closed, the switch should be returned to neutral.

WARNING

Since the hydraulic lines to the speed brake actuating cylinders are routed near the engine, it is extremely important that the speed brake switch be kept in the neutral position to minimize the fire hazard should a line be damaged.

LANDING GEAR

GENERAL

57 The landing gear and wheel fairing doors are hydraulically actuated and electrically controlled and sequenced. A removable ground safety lock may be inserted in the nose gear assembly to prevent inadvertent nose gear retraction on the ground. No ground safety locks are provided for the main gear, as the weight of the aircraft on the main gear prevents accidental retraction while the aircraft is motionless.

NORMAL LANDING GEAR CONTROL

58 A landing gear control handle at the left side of the instrument panel electrically controls the landing gear and door hydraulic selector valves. The control handle has two positions: UP and DOWN. When the gear is down and locked and the weight of the aircraft is on the gear, a ground safety switch prevents retraction if the gear handle is inadvertently moved to UP. The fairing doors are not controlled by this switch and will follow their normal sequence, opening when the gear control is moved to UP, thereby providing warning to the ground crew that the gear control is in the wrong position for taxiing.

LANDING GEAR EMERGENCY UP CONTROL

59 If it is necessary to collapse the gear in an emergency, the landing gear ground safety switch can be overridden by use of a shielded EMERG UP push-button switch located above the gear control handle. When the gear control is at UP and the EMERG UP button is depressed, the ground safety switch and the landing gear door solenoid are by-passed and the gear is retracted hydraulically in the normal manner, except that the fairing doors will not open and will be damaged by retraction of the gear.

LANDING GEAR EMERGENCY RELEASE

60 When the landing gear emergency release at the bottom of the centre pedestal, see Figure 1-9, is pulled all the way out and held for at least 11 seconds, the main gear and all the fairing doors are mechanically unlocked and the gear and door hydraulic selector valves are positioned to lower the gear. If the electrical

control system has failed, the gear will lower under pressure from the main hydraulic system. If the hydraulic system has failed, the main gear will fall free when the emergency release is pulled.

WARNING

Whenever the landing gear emergency lowering system has been used, the nose gear cannot be retracted in flight. It will be necessary to manually reset the nose gear emergency lowering valve on the ground. This will automatically charge the accumulator by utility system pressure.

LANDING GEAR POSITION INDICATORS

61 The position of the landing gear is shown by three indicators on the left forward console, see Figure 1-10. One indicator is provided for each gear and will display parallel red and yellow diagonal lines if its respective gear is in an unlocked condition. The diagonal lines will also appear when the battery-starter switch is OFF or when primary bus is not energized. The word UP appears if the gear is up and locked. A miniature wheel shows when the gear is down and locked.

LANDING GEAR WARNING HORN

62 When the throttle is retarded below cruising power, a warning horn in the cockpit sounds if the landing gear is not down and locked. A horn cut-out button is located on the left forward console.

LANDING GEAR CONTROL WARNING LIGHT

63 A red warning light is located within the landing gear control handle. The light may be tested by pressing the warning horn cut-out button with the throttle in the retarded position. The light illuminates under the following conditions.

(a) With the handle UP and any gear or door unlocked.

(b) With the handle DOWN and any gear unlocked.

(c) With the handle UP, the gear and doors locked up, and the throttle retarded below minimum cruising rpm.

NOSE WHEEL STEERING SYSTEM

64 The nose wheel steering system is electrically engaged, hydraulically powered and controlled by the rudder pedals. Steering is accomplished by depressing a switch on the stick grip, synchronizing the rudder pedals with the nose wheel, and then operating the rudder pedals to control a hydraulically-operated nose wheel steering unit. This unit permits the wheel to be turned approximately 21° each side of centre. When not engaged for steering, the unit serves as a conventional hydraulic shimmy damper. A safety switch, mounted on the nose wheel strut torque link, prevents engagement of the steering unit whenever the weight of the aircraft is off the nose gear.

NOSE WHEEL TOWING RELEASE PIN

65 The nose wheel towing release pin is located on the left side of the nose gear strut just above the wheel fork. For towing the aircraft, the pin is disengaged, disconnecting the steering damper unit and allowing the wheel to swivel. Before flight, make sure the safety cap is on. This will ensure that the release pin is engaged.

NOSE WHEEL STEERING SWITCH

66 The push-button type nose wheel steering switch on the stick grip actuates a shut-off valve to supply hydraulic pressure to the nose gear steering unit. To engage the steering unit the switch must be depressed and the rudder pedals synchronized with the nose wheel. When the nose wheel and rudder pedals are co-ordinated in this manner, the nose wheel steering unit is automatically engaged. The unit will not engage if the nose wheel is more than 21° either side of centre. Should the nose wheel be turned more than this, it must be brought within the steering range by use of the wheel brakes.

WHEEL BRAKES

GENERAL

67 The wheel brakes are operated by toe action on the rudder pedals. Brake pressure is supplied from brake master cylinders supplemented by power boost from the utility hydraulic system. If no pressure is available from the utility hydraulic system, the brakes function through conventional action of the brake master cylinders when toe pressure is applied to the rudder pedals, but greater effort is required for a given effect.

PARKING BRAKE CONTROL

68 The parking brake handle is located on the left side of the cockpit, above and outboard of the landing gear control. Parking brakes are set by pressing hard on the toe brakes, pulling the parking brake handle all the way out, releasing toe brake pressure and releasing the parking brake handle. Parking brakes are released by exerting pressure on the toe brakes. If brakes do not release easily, the toe brakes should be pressed hard and the parking brake handle pushed all the way in.

CAUTION

To avoid the possibility of brake malfunction, ensure that the parking brake handle is pushed fully in before taxiing. To prevent seizing, allow the wheel brakes to cool after taxiing, before setting the parking brake.

POWER PLANT CONTROL SYSTEM

MAIN FUEL CONTROL SYSTEM

69 The fuel system consists of two engine-driven, variable-delivery pumps, proportional flow control unit, acceleration control unit, jet pipe temperature (JPT) limiter, non-return valves, flow distributor, minimum pressure valve and dump valve. Engine requirements are sensed through a servo mechanism which controls the fuel pump delivery according to various throttle openings. Ram pressure and varying altitudes are also a controlling factor. Each pump is capable of delivering suffic fuel to ensure rated thrust, depending temperature and type of fuel.

EMERGENCY FUEL SYSTEM

70 The emergency fuel system provides manual control of the fuel flow in the ever failure of one of the fuel pumps or malfunc of the automatic flow control units. When emergency fuel control switch on the instrument panel is placed ON, the fuel flov directed through a separate emergency control unit to the flow distributor, by-pass the proportional flow control unit, accelerat control unit and JPT limiter. The servo syst is isolated and the fuel pumps deliver output at all engine speeds up to governing r

CAUTION

When operating on the emergency fuel system, all accelerations are manually controlled and it is essential that a slow, steady movement of the throttle be maintained.

EMERGENCY FUEL CONTROL SWITCH

71 A two-position switch on the upper side of the instrument panel, when placed C directs the flow from the engine fuel pum through the emergency fuel system. A warn light indicates when the switch is ON.

LOW FUEL PRESSURE WARNING LIGHT

72 A warning light on the instrument pa indicates when the fuel pressure drops approximately 3 psi.

JET PIPE TEMPERATURE VARIATION

73 The jet pipe temperature of engin with fixed area exhaust nozzles is affected ambient air temperature, altitude, airspe and rpm. Generally, with constant altitude a rpm, JPT will increase with ambient air ter perature above 5°C (41°F) or with airspeed. will increase with altitude up to approximate 20,000 feet. These factors can change sing or coincidentally, thus causing an inconsiste JPT for any given rpm. Ordinarily, an increa in JPT can be expected during take-off, and on the climb to approximately 20,000 feet, up to (715° ± 15°C), (1319° ± 59°F) when it will be controlled by the JPT limiter. Control by the JPT limiter with the throttle lever at the normal full throttle stop, will result in a drop in engine speed. The engine speed will continue to drop as altitude is increased.

74 No action can be taken by the pilot if jet pipe temperature is below the limit, although it should be remembered that thrust decreases with a decrease in JPT during operation at a constant engine rpm. Jet pipe temperatures are automatically controlled, when using normal engine fuel system, by the incorporation of a limiter system which does not allow the temperature to exceed approximately 715° (±15°C), (1319° ± 59°F). The limiter is inoperative when operating on the emergency fuel system.

THROTTLE CONTROL LEVER

75 The throttle control lever, see Figure 1-11 is linked to the throttle valves on the proportional flow control and emergency flow control units. With the engine master switch ON, initial outboard movement of the throttle lever energizes the fuel booster pump and the ignition circuits. When the throttle lever is advanced from OFF to IDLE, fuel flow for idling is maintained by a by-pass from the throttle valve. Closing the throttle lever cuts off the idling flow, thus obviating the necessity for a separate high pressure shut-off cock. A stop is fitted to the quadrant at the IDLE position to prevent inadvertent shutting off of the fuel supply. This stop may be by-passed when starting or stopping the engine. The grip on the throttle lever contains the speed brake switch, the gunsight, gyro caging button and the microphone button. Rotation of the grip will manually range the radar gunsight. The normal full throttle stop may be overridden in an emergency by moving the throttle lever outboard and advancing it to the end of the quadrant. This action will override the JPT limiter and at the same time will break the wire tell-tale. (Refer to Part 3).

ENGINE MASTER SWITCH

76 The shielded engine master switch on the right console, see Figure 1-12, controls the low pressure fuel shut-off valve and completes the electrical circuits to the fuel booster pumps and to the throttle lever actuated micro-switch controlling ignition during starting.

IGNITION

77 Current for ignition is supplied to the spark plugs when the engine master and starter switches are ON and the throttle lever is moved from the OFF position. When the starter is subsequently disconnected from the circuit the ignition relay is de-energized. Ignition is required only during the starting procedure, since the mixture in the combustion chambers will burn continuously after being ignited.

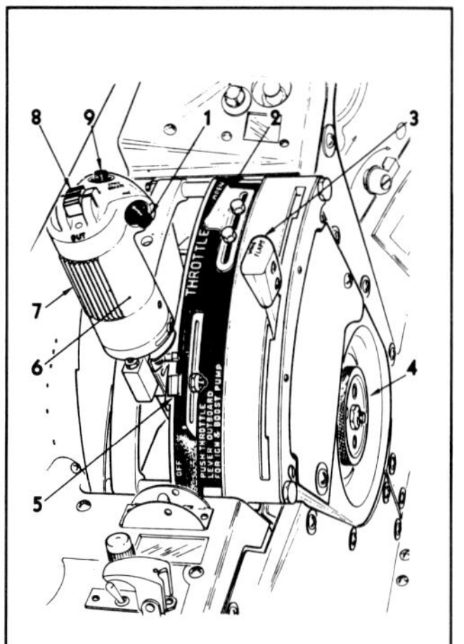

1 MICROPHONE BUTTON
2 JET PIPE TEMPERATURE LIMITER OVERRIDE STOP
3 WING FLAP LEVER
4 THROTTLE LEVER FRICTION WHEEL
5 IDLE STOP
6 THROTTLE CONTROL LEVER
7 RADAR GUNSIGHT MANUAL RANGE CONTROL
8 SPEED BRAKE SWITCH
9 GYRO GUNSIGHT CAGING BUTTON

Figure 1-11 Throttle Control Lever

EMERGENCY IGNITION SWITCH

78 A duplicate air start ignition switch is installed on upper left hand corner of instrument panel to enable the pilot to operate the emergency ignition and emergency fuel switches simultaneously with his left hand. The switches are located, one on right forward console, see Figure 1-12, and the other one on a bracket at the upper left hand corner of the instrument panel, see Figure 1-2. These switches are used to supply ignition for re-starting the engine in flight. With the emergency ignition switch on (forward), the batter is connected to the ignition system when the throttle lever is advanced from OFF and th battery switch is ON. The emergency ignition switch should be left on only until ignitio occurs, as it causes an additional drain or the battery. If the switch is left on for longe than three minutes or is used too frequently the ignition transformer will be damaged

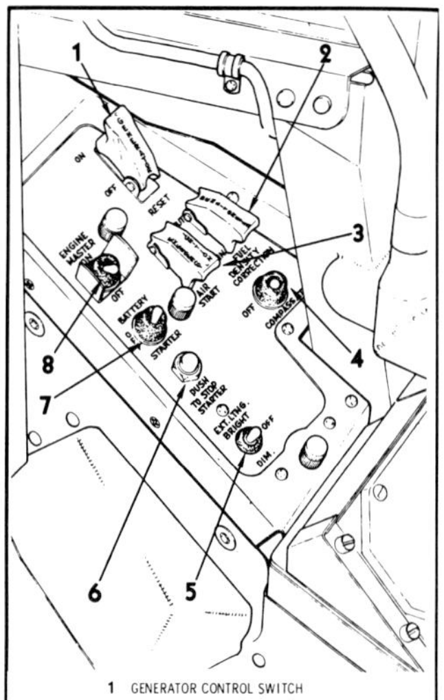

1 GENERATOR CONTROL SWITCH
2 FUEL DENSITY CORRECTION SWITCH
3 EMERGENCY IGNITION SWITCH
4 STANDBY COMPASS LIGHT SWITCH
5 EXTERIOR LIGHTS SWITCH
6 PUSH-TO-STOP-STARTER BUTTON
7 BATTERY-STARTER SWITCH
8 ENGINE MASTER SWITCH

5E1A-01-16C

Figure 1-12 Right Forward Console

STARTER

79 A combination starter-generator unit is provided for cranking the engine. An external power source must be used for starting, as the starter cannot be powered by the aircraft battery. The battery-starter switch on the engine control panel operates the starter when held momentarily at the STARTER position. A starter relay continues to energize the starter until engine speed reaches the required rpm at which point the starter circuit is automatically disconnected.

PUSH-TO-STOP-STARTER BUTTON

80 A button, marked PUSH TO STOP STARTER, is located below the battery starter switch on the right forward console. During the normal starting procedure, this button is used to de-energize the starter if the engine fails to start and also to prevent damage to the starter if the starter cut-out fails to operate.

FLIGHT AND ENGINE INSTRUMENTS

FLIGHT INSTRUMENTS

81 The following flight instruments are provided: altimeter, airspeed indicator, vertical speed indicator, turn and bank indicator artificial horizon, gyro compass, magnetic compass, radio compass, accelerometer, machmeter, clock and cabin altimeter.

GYRO COMPASS FAST SLAVING BUTTON

82 The gyro compass fast slaving button located on the instrument panel de-energizes the slow slaving cycle to permit faster gyro recovery to the tube heading. When the primary bus is powered for starting purposes, the gyro compass is automatically on a fast slaving cycle for the first two or three minutes, making operation of the fast slaving button unnecessary.

STARTING PROCEDURE

...ORE STARTING

External power, supplied through both ...ptacles, must be used for starting, as the ...ry does not supply power to the starter. ...re that the energizer is functioning cor-...y, is properly connected to the aircraft, ...t at 28.5 volts and is selected to GROUND ...ER.

WARNING

...ake sure danger areas fore and aft of ...ircraft are clear of personnel, aircraft ...nd vehicles, see Figure 2-2. Suction ...t the intake duct is sufficient to kill or ...eriously injure personnel if they are ...rawn into or against the duct. Danger ...t of the aircraft is created by the high ...et pipe temperature and blast from the ...ail-pipe. Whenever practicable, start ...nd run up engine on a concrete surface ...o minimize the possibility of dirt and ...oreign objects being drawn into the

craft headed into or at right angles to the wind as jet pipe temperature may be increased or an engine fire aggravated by a tail wind.

STARTING

6 To perform a normal start, proceed as follows:

(a) Check that ignition circuit-breaker is in.

(b) Place engine master switch ON.

(c) Place throttle lever outboard.

(d) Check that low fuel pressure warning light goes out.

NOTE

Operation of the engine under conditions of low inlet fuel pressure to the engine-driven fuel pumps (causing the fuel pressure warning light to be on) must not exceed a total of 30 minutes between pump overhauls. The periods should be recorded on the L14A.

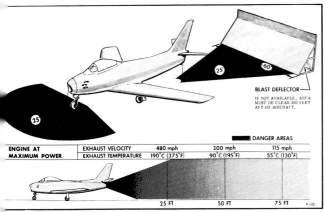

ENGINE AT MAXIMUM POWER:

EXHAUST VELOCITY	480 mph	200 mph	115 mph
EXHAUST TEMPERATURE	190°C (375°F)	90°C (195°F)	55°C (130°F)

BLAST DEFLECTOR — IF NOT AVAILABLE, AREA MUST BE CLEAR 200 FEET AFT OF AIRCRAFT.

■ DANGER AREAS

25 FT 50 FT 75 FT

Figure 2-2 Danger Areas

(e) Hold the battery-starter switch in STARTER position for three seconds, then move to BATTERY.

CAUTION

The high starting current will quickly burn out the starter if the engine does not begin to turn as soon as the starter is engaged. If there is no audible indication of engine rotation or if the tachometer fails to register within three seconds, depress the push-to-stop-starter button immediately.

(f) At a minimum of 9% engine rpm, advance the throttle to IDLE.

CAUTION

Do not advance throttle past the IDLE stop. If a minimum of 9% rpm is not obtained within 45 seconds, abandon start by pressing push-to-stop-starter button and place aircraft unserviceable.

NOTE

An audible report in the combustion chambers and a large exhaust flame may be experienced when starting the engine. This is a normal occurrence.

(g) At approximately 30% rpm, depress the push-to-stop-starter button. Engine motoring period should not exceed 45 seconds.

(h) Check that the engine accelerates to idling speed and stays there (34% to 39%).

(j) Check that jet pipe temperature does not exceed 850°C (1562°F) at any time.

(k) Have external power disconnected after engine has reached idling rpm.

FALSE START

7 If, during the normal starting sequence, the throttle is advanced to idle and there is no noticeable rise in jet pipe temperature within ten seconds, proceed as follows:

(a) Retard throttle to the OFF position.

(b) Allow engine to complete 45-second motoring cycle to clear excess fuel.

(c) Press the push-to-stop-starter button.

(d) Allow engine to run down to a stand still.

(e) Place engine master switch OFF.

(f) Place battery switch OFF.

(g) Investigate cause of failure to light up.

(h) When cause has been ascertained and rectified, motor engine for 40 seconds to blow out excess fuel if evident.

(j) Allow at least 1-1/2 minutes after engine has stopped rotating before attempting to restart.

NOTE

A maximum of two repeated cycles of 45 seconds each is permissible. A cooling period of at least 90 minutes must then elapse before attempting further starts.

HOT START

8 If, during the normal starting sequence, the jet pipe temperature exceeds 850°C (1562°F) proceed as follows:

(a) Retard throttle to the OFF position immediately.

(b) Press the push-to-stop-starter button.

(c) Allow engine to run down to a standstill.

(d) Place engine master switch OFF.

(e) Place battery switch OFF.

(f) Investigate cause of hot start. Do not attempt a restart until cause has been ascertained.

NOTE

All hot starts, and the period of excessive temperature, must be recorded in the engine log book. When five starts

---

of 850°C (1562°F) or above have been recorded, the engine must be removed for a hot-end inspection.

GROUND TESTS

...ENERAL

No engine warm-up is necessary. As ...oon as the engine stabilizes at idling speed ...ith normal gauge readings, the throttle may ...e opened to full power. After engine is started, ...heck the following:

CAUTION

If a full power engine run-up is made during ground tests, be sure wheels are chocked and brakes are held on.

...a) Check that engine idling rpm is between ...4% and 39%.

...b) Check that jet pipe temperature does ...ot exceed 540°C (1004°F).

...c) Check that oil pressure at idling rpm ...s at least 2 psi.

...d) Check engine instruments for desired readings.

(e) Check flight control hydraulic systems as follows:

(1) Hold flight control switch in RESET momentarily (one second) to engage normal flight control system. Check alternate light goes out.

(2) With flight control switch and the hydraulic pressure gauge selector switch in NORMAL, move control column and visually check control surfaces movement. Check pressure returns to normal range of 2550 to 3200 psi.

(3) Operate ailerons and elevators to reduce normal pressure and check that alternate light comes on when normal pressure is between 960 and 540 psi. Normal pressure should then build up to 3000 (+160-60) psi.

(4) Place hydraulic pressure gauge selector switch in ALTERNATE and check that

pressure cycles between 2550 and 3200 psi. Pump the control column slightly to verify that alternate system is operating.

(5) Hold flight control switch in RESET momentarily (one second) and check that alternate light goes out and normal system is operating.

(f) Check the utility hydraulic system by running speed brakes through one complete cycle and, with the hydraulic pressure gauge selector switch at UTILITY, check pressure indicated on the gauge.

CAUTION

Before operating speed brakes, be sure area around speed brakes is clear, as brakes operate rapidly and forcefully, and can injure personnel.

(g) Gunsight on.

(h) At 45% engine rpm, check electrical loadmeter reading. Check voltmeter for approximately 28 (±0.5) volts. (Generator will not operate below approximately 23% rpm).

TAXIING

GENERAL

10 Directional control of the aircraft is maintained through the steerable nose wheel by means of the rudder pedals. Nose wheel and rudder pedal position must be co-ordinated before steering mechanism will engage and the steering switch must be held depressed at all times while taxiing.

11 Before commencing to taxi, proceed as follows:

(a) Signal for removal of wheel chocks,

(b) Check parking brakes off. Depress toe pedals and check that parking brake handle is fully in.

12 Observe the following instructions for taxiing.

(a) Once the aircraft is moving, taxi at the lowest practical rpm.

(b) Avoid excessive or rapid jockeying of the throttle while taxiing.

(c) Minimize taxi time, as aircraft range is considerably reduced by high fuel consumption during taxiing.

CAUTION

Nose wheel steering becomes ineffective during speed brake cycling if speed brakes are operated whilst taxiing.

TAKE-OFF PROCEDURES

VITAL ACTIONS BEFORE TAKE-OFF

13 Just prior to take-off, complete the following checks:

H - Hydraulic - Pressure 3000 (+160 - 60) psi.

　　Harness and safety belt - Tightened. Lockhandle unlocked.

T - Trim - Set for take-off.

F - Fuel - Sufficient for flight.

　　Flaps - One-half down, Speed brakes IN.

G - Gyros Erected.

S - Switches - Generator ON.

　　- Engine master ON.

　　- Battery-starter switch BATTERY.

　　- Instrument power NORM.

　　- Bomb release selector switch AUTO RELEASE.

　　- All other armament switches OFF.

NOTE

To jettison drop tanks or other external stores during take-off, use bomb-rocket-tank jettison button.

O - Oxygen - Checked and NORMAL.

C - Canopy - Closed.

P - Pitot heat (wing and duct) - As required.

14 Taxi to take-off position, heading aircraft straight down runway with nose wheel centered.

TAKE-OFF

15 Use the following procedure for take-off.

(a) Move throttle fully forward. Check that rpm obtained is 100 (+0.5 -1.0)% and JPT is normally (715° ± 15°C) (1319° ± 59°F). Take-off may proceed, however, if JPT is not less than 660°C (1220°F).

(b) Release brakes and begin take-off run.

(c) Maintain directional control by using nose wheel steering until rudder control becomes effective.

(d) With a gross weight of 15,000 pounds and a clean aircraft, the nose wheel lift-off speed is 100 knots and take-off speed 115 knots.

(e) With a gross weight of 18,000 pounds and two 167 Imperial gallon drop tanks, nose wheel lift-off speed is 110 knots and take-off speed 125 knots.

(f) A nose-high attitude must be maintained for take-off. After take-off, the aircraft will assume a more normal attitude as airspeed increases and flaps are raised.

(g) Refer to Take-off Chart in Part 4, for required take-off distances.

16 Refer to Part 3, for procedure in case of engine failure during take-off.

17 When the aircraft is definitely airborne, proceed as follows:

(a) Landing gear handle UP. Approximately eight seconds required for gear retraction.

(b) Wing flaps UP immediately after landing gear handle UP. No sink will occur because of the rapid acceleration of the aircraft. When flaps are full up, the flap lever may be left in the UP position or returned to the HOLD position.

CAUTION

Aircraft speed must be kept below 185 knots IAS until the flaps are fully raised and the gear is locked up, otherwise excessive airloads may damage gear operating mechanism and prevent subsequent extension of gear. If flaps do not fully retract, avoid high speed and high G pull-ups. Failure of the flap actuating mechanism may occur if the flaps are not supported against the up-stop (fully retracted) during accelerated manoeuvres at high speed. If flaps are left down or accidentally lowered over 185 knots, leave them extended and avoid high speed. Land as soon as possible.

NOTE

To allow for the more rapid acceleration due to increased thrust during cold weather operation, the initial climb angle should be steepened, so that the placard limit speed for gear and flaps extended will not be exceeded before retraction is complete.

(c) Trim horizontal tail as required.

(d) Level off and accelerate immediately to best climbing speed. Refer to Part 4, for climb data.

CLIMB

GENERAL

18 Climb at take-off rpm (time limit - 15 minutes at 720°C (1328°F) or limiter temperature, 30 minutes at 685°C (1265°F) JPT). Refer to Climb Charts in Part 4 for recommended indicated airspeed to be used during climb and for rates of climb and fuel consumption.

DURING FLIGHT

GENERAL

19 The aircraft must be frequently and accurately trimmed to maintain maximum aerodynamic efficiency.

NOTE

The elevator and aileron trim switch installed on the type B-8 stick grip is designed to return to the neutral position automatically when thumb pressure is released after actuating the switch. Experience has shown that is is possible for this switch to remain in the actuated position, causing an overtrim condition. To prevent this, the switch should be manually returned to the neutral position.

ENGINE OPERATION

20 Observe the following engine operating instructions:

(a) To check for normally functioning JPT Limiter.

(1) In the full throttle climb, rpm will begin at 15-20,000 feet, with the JPT holding at the Limiter setting. If held at full throttle to 40,000 feet, rpm will have reduced 1 to 3%.

(2) To check at 40,000 feet, cruise 2 minutes at 95%. Open to full throttle and hold for 2 minutes. In a few seconds rpm will begin to reduce and in less than 2 minutes should be 1 to 3% below the normal ground level governor setting. The JPT should hold at the Limiter setting.

(3) If a check of the Limiter over-ride is made this should not be held for more than 10 to 15 seconds. The rpm may rise to 102% and JPT to as high as 760°C (1400°F).

(b) Retard throttle control to the desired setting (Refer to Flight Operation Instruction Charts in Part 4 for cruise data).

(c) Periodically check for desired instrument readings.

WARNING

If the oil pressure drops below 14 psi at engine speeds of 75% rpm and above, or if it fluctuates more than 4 psi continually, return to base immediately.

HYDRAULIC SYSTEM FLIGHT CHECK

21 Check hydraulic systems periodically as follows:

(a) Place pressure gauge selector at UTILITY and read gauge for proper utility system pressure.

(b) Fly straight and level for 30 seconds. With the gauge selector switch at NORMAL, read pressure gauge for flight control normal system pressure.

(c) Without moving control column and with gauge selector switch at ALTERNATE, read gauge for flight control alternate hydraulic system pressure.

(d) Check flight control alternate hydraulic system operation as follows: Place the flight control switch at ALTERNATE ON and check operation of the horizontal tail and the ailerons, Hold the switch at RESET momentarily (one second) and then release. System will then return to NORMAL.

FLYING CHARACTERISTICS

GENERAL

22 The hydraulic flight control system is considerably more sensitive than conventional control systems. Until experience is gai handling the increased power of the sy large or abrupt control movements shou avoided. Two completely independent hyd flight control systems are provided as a feature in case one of the systems is dan in combat.

23 Inverted flying or any manoeuvre results in negative G must be limited to seconds duration, as there is no means o suring a continuous flow of fuel due to sta tion of the fuel booster pumps.

24 With the slatted wing leading edges resultant changes in flight characteristics improved stability, improved low speed c acteristics with better lateral stability, red stall speeds and improved manoeuvrabili high altitudes.

LOW-SPEED STALL

25 The stall, with gear and flaps dowr preceded by a light, general aircraft b about 10 knots above the stall and a ru buffet of medium intensity just before the s For normal stalling speeds, see Figure

Gear and Flaps Down. Speed in knots IAS.					
	Fuel in pounds	Nose Gear lift-off	Take-off	Power-off stall	Final approac
Clean	Full fuel	100	115	104	140
	1500			99	135
	500			95	130
Two 100 Imperial Gallon Tanks	Full fuel	105	120	110	150
	1500*			99	135
	500*			95	130
Two 167 Imperial Gallon Tanks	Full fuel	110	125	114	160
	1500*			100	135
	500*			96	130

*All external fuel used. Empty tanks retained. Ammunition or ballast aboard.

Figure 2-3 Stall Speeds

HIGH-SPEED ACCELERATED STALLS

26 An accelerated or high-speed stall below approximately 25,000 feet can damage the aircraft or cause pilot black-out and consequent loss of control. As the aircraft approaches a high-speed stall, there is considerable airframe buffeting, which may cause severe stress and possible structural damage. This buffet onset gives ample warning to permit relaxation of back pressure and thus avoid the stall, Abrupt use of elevators should be avoided, especially during speed brake opening, (refer to para. 37 following).

SPINS

27 The aircraft shows normal spin characteristics during spin entry, sustained spin and recovery. Spins are initiated in the normal manner. They may vary between spins to the left and spins to the right, and in some cases it may be impossible to properly spin the aircraft at all. In a fully developed spin, the nose rises and falls slowly during each turn, which takes about four seconds and about 2000 feet of height. Buffeting occurs and usually decreases as the spin progresses. A non-oscillatory type spin may be encountered. The nose of the aircraft will not rise and fall through each turn; instead, the aircraft will spin rapidly with a steady pitch angle. This type of spin usually requires more turns for recovery after corrective action is taken.

SPIN RECOVERY

28 To recover from a spin proceed as follows:

(a) Reduce throttle to IDLE rpm, retract flaps and landing gear, and close speed brakes.

(b) After determining the direction of rotation by reference to the turn indicator, apply full opposite rudder.

(c) Move the control column slowly forward until the spin stops. Do not push the control fully forward as this is not necessary and will only result in an excessively steep recovery attitude, possibly beyond the vertical.

(d) Keep ailerons neutral.

(e) Centralize rudder as soon as spin stops.

(f) Gently ease out of the resulting dive. Be sure to regain flying speed before opening speed brakes or pulling up, or the aircraft will stall and snap into another spin.

NOTE

If in a non-oscillatory type spin, maintain standard recovery control for a minimum of three turns, ensuring that ailerons are neutral and that the control column is neutral or slightly forward. If spin does not stop, hold recovery control and apply power.

29 Actual tests have shown that this procedure applies to the following configurations:

(a) Clean aircraft, speed brakes in or out, right or left hand spins.

(b) With 100 Imperial gallon drop tanks empty, speed brakes in or out, right or left hand spins.

NOTE

Although spins with external armament stores and 100 or 167 Imperial gallon tanks are prohibited, recovery from inadvertent spins can be made as outlined but may require up to three turns. If at this time recovery is not successful and altitude permits, jettison stores and repeat normal recovery action, which should be effective in 1/4 to 1 turn.

MINIMUM ALTITUDE FOR SPIN RECOVERY

30 Flight tests indicate that 7000 feet is required to complete recovery from a one-turn spin plus a one-turn recovery and a 4G pullout. The altitude loss during this manoeuvre will be about 6500 feet. In a spin below 10,000 feet bail out, since the margin of safety is too small to try a recovery.

INVERTED SPINS

31 Two types of inverted spins may be encountered in this aircraft. The first is characterized by a roll upright into a 45° dive attitude approximately every three-fourths turn, followed by a roll again into the inverted spin position, repeating the initial spin. Each turn takes approximately six seconds. Recovery can be initiated at any time by neutralizing the controls and dropping the nose as the aircraft rolls upright.

32 The second type spin is entered from an extreme nose-up angle followed by the nose dropping through to some 80° below the horizon and the aircraft rolling to an inverted position with the wings approximately horizontal. Complete pilot disorientation results from this type of spin, causing the pilot to take incorrect recovery action. The direction of rotation in the spin can only be determined by reference to the turn indicator. Recovery action is to establish first the direction of rotation by reference to the turn indicator, then carry out the normal recovery action.

NOTE

Although inverted spin recovery is described, it is improbable that such a condition will be encountered.

PILOT-INDUCED OSCILLATION (PORPOISING)

33 Occasionally an over-control manoeuvre may be induced, consisting of a rapid up-and-down pitching of porpoising motion. The tendency is to induce this manoeuvre at low altitudes. It is usually initiated by pushing over to zero or negative G too rapidly or by attempting to correct too rapidly for a trim change such as caused by a gust, speed brake operation or rapid throttle movement. The magnitude of the oscillation will depend upon how rapidly and how much corrective control is applied.

34 The oscillation is basically caused by a combination of applied stick forces, control column displacement and the inherent longitudinal response characteristics of the aircraft. Pilot-applied boosts sustain the oscillation and this is further aggravated by the effects of G upon the pilot, throwing his weight up and down as well as fore and aft, sustaining the oscillation through inadvertent control column movements. The quickest way to damp the oscillation is to release the control column. The oscillation will damp in approximately one cycle. It may also be stopped by makin a slow, positive pull-up to approximately 3 while attempting to maintain a steady bac pressure. The oscillation will not damp ou quite as fast for the positive pull-up metho as for the control release method.

NOTE

Do not try to stop the oscillation by attempting to push the control column fore and aft in opposition to the motion. This will only aggravate the condition, since the motion is too rapid to estimate and apply corrections.

HIGH ALTITUDE PILOT OVERCONTROL

35 An overcontrol manoeuvre consisting of erratic up-and-down pitching can be induced at high altitudes. It may be found difficult to fly close formation at high altitudes due to unintentionally overcontrolling the aircraft. The resulting oscillation is not violent but is objectionable because of the constant necessity for corrective control. To minimize this overcontrol manoeuvre when flying formation, adhere to recommended climb and cruise schedules, since the oscillation becomes less pronounced as Mach is increased.

AILERON CONTROL

36 Until familiar with aileron effectiveness at high speeds, care should be taken not to overcontrol in making abrupt or consecutive rolls. Refer to Part 4 for restrictions with external stores. Should failure of the normal flight control system occur, automatic change-over to the alternate system is provided instantaneously with no reduction in effect of aileron control or increase in pilot effort.

USE OF SPEED BRAKES

37 To reduce speed, especially in aerobatics or formation flight, speed brakes may be used without objectionable buffeting or uncontrollable changes in trim. In a pull-out, recovery may be effected with minimum altitude loss by first opening the speed brakes and then pulling out a maximum permissible G. Opening the speed brakes without applying elevator control results in an automatic pitch-up of up to 3G, the actual amount of pitching depending on the airspeed.

...cept in extreme emergencies, do not
...ll the control column back during the
...ne the speed brakes are opening. To
...so may result in exceeding the load
...ctor limit. The speed brakes open
...lly in approximately two seconds.

...SE SPEED

In the medium-to-high speed range,
... flight handling characteristics are con-
...red good about all three axes. For those
...stomed to conventional elevator control,
...more effective stabilizer may appear con-
...rably more sensitive because of the faster
...tion to small control column movements.
...advisable not to attempt close flight in
...nation until accustomed to the control.
...imum available rate of roll is quite high
...ll altitudes. The aircraft is most sen-
...e to small fore-and-aft control movements
...ween Mach 0.8 and Mach 0.9 at low
...udes.

HIGH SPEED

39 Stability and control are unaffected by
compressibility up to approximately Mach 0.95
with the exception of a slight flattening tendency
in the stick force gradient for 1G flight between
Mach 0.85 and Mach 0.90. The aircraft nose-up
tendency which appears in this high-speed
region requires steadily increasing forward
control column movement to increase the speed
of the aircraft. As in other speed ranges, use
of the stabilizer results in quite positive
and immediate reaction. The power of the
controllable horizontal tail will become particularly noticeable above 500 knots, especially
in turbulent air. Based on structural design
limits, a limit airspeed of 600 knots, or the
airspeed where wing roll becomes excessive,
has been established. This limit has been
imposed because wing heaviness, although
easily controllable at high altitude, may become a limiting condition at lower altitudes.

AILERON AERODYNAMIC LOCK

40 At altitudes below 40,000 feet, pull-out
acceleration greater than 2G combined with

speeds higher than Mach 0.95 can produce
aerodynamic loads in excess of power available
in aileron jacks, resulting in aileron locking.
Recovery from a dive at speeds in excess of
Mach 0.95 should be initiated at a sufficiently
high altitude to ensure that speed is reduced
below Mach 0.95 before reaching 25,000 feet,
unless speed is reduced by dive brakes or
throttle adjustment.

Aileron trim should not be applied when
ailerons are locked, as this may result
in a severe rolling manoeuvre when
aileron control is restored.

TURNING RADIUS CONTROL

41 Turning radius varies directly with airspeed and altitude, an increase in either
resulting in a wider turn. The most important
factor in turning radius control is reduction in
airspeed. This can be effected in two ways.
One method is to exchange the excess speed for
altitude by making a sharp climbing turn. The
alternative is to open the speed brakes,
remembering to reduce control column pressure simultaneously with speed brake opening
in order to maintain the same G. If forward
control is not applied with speed brake opening,
the aircraft may stall at high altitudes or may
exceed the limit G at low altitudes. Conversely,
a backward control movement is necessary
when closing the brakes to maintain the same
G. When using either method of reducing speed,
be careful not to let the airspeed fall below
the best climb speed. Tighter turns may be
made at high altitudes with the slat-equipped
aircraft because more G may be applied before
the stall. The onset of buffet may commence
at a lower G loading, but, once the slats have
opened, the magnitude of the buffet is reduced.

LETDOWN

42 Normally, the most economical letdown
with a clean aircraft is at Mach 0.8 with a
throttle setting which allows minimum operating jet pipe temperature. Emergency letdown
rates of descent as high as 27,000 feet per
minute can be obtained by closing the throttle,
opening the speed brakes and diving to maintain
Mach 0.95.

RECOMMENDED SPEED FOR MINIMUM RADIUS TURNS

43 Although minimum radius turns can be
achieved at low Mach, it is better not to let
the speed drop below that for best climb.
This would place the aircraft in a speed range
where acceleration to higher speeds is very
difficult without loss of height. The same
information applies to diving turns made at
maximum G at constant Mach. Note also that
the high-speed manoeuvring essential in combat
will lead to larger turning radii.

G-LIMIT OVERSHOOT

44 A basic characteristic towards longitudinal instability under conditions of high load
factor, which is experienced during a turn or
pull-up, results in a tendency to automatically
increase the rate of turn or pull-up to a point
where the limit load factor may be exceeded.
This is termed over-shoot. The approach to
this condition can usually be recognized by a
distinct increase in aircraft buffeting, which
should be treated as a warning that the
manoeuvre is becoming critical. This applies
under all conditions of altitude, Mach, gross
weight or configuration, but the use of the
stabilizer as a primary control surface makes
immediate and effective recovery action
possible before the aircraft exceeds its limit
G load.

(a) When encountering the buffet boundary,
check the rate of turn or pull-up, and be
prepared to apply further preventative control
against overshoot condition, and possible
resultant damage to the aircraft, see Figure
2-4.

(b) The aircraft is limited to stated load
factors, (refer to Load Factor Limit Tables,
in Part 4). Never deliberately exceed these
limits.

DIVE RECOVERY

45 Because of aircraft trim changes which
occur during pull-ups at high Mach, the following procedure is recommended for recovery
from high Mach dives or manoeuvres.

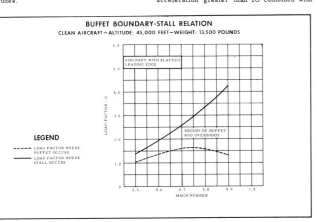

BUFFET BOUNDARY-STALL RELATION
CLEAN AIRCRAFT — ALTITUDE: 45,000 FEET — WEIGHT: 13,500 POUNDS

Figure 2-4 Buffet Boundary - Stall Relation

Open the speed brakes. Do not move
...control column back until after speed brakes
...ve opened and the nose up reaction to brake
...ension has developed.

... Apply backward pressure as necessary
...effect the desired pull-out, see Figure 2-5.

...NG HEAVINESS

At a speed of approximately Mach 0.9
...e aircraft becomes one-wing heavy. Either
...ng may tend to drop but aileron control is
...fficient to counteract it.

...LIGHT STRENGTH DIAGRAM

... The Flight Strength Diagram, see Figure
...-6, describes the strength limitations of the
...ean aircraft for symmetrical manoeuvres.
...he left boundary lines, marked for various
...titudes, show indicated stalling speeds under
...arious load factor conditions from +7G to -3G.
...or other conditions, such as an asymmetrical

or rolling pull-out and external load, refer to
Load Factor Limits Table in Part 4, following.

NOTE

If the accelerometer records Gs in
excess of those specified for any particular flight condition in the Load Factor
Limits Table, have the aircraft in-
spected after landing for signs of
structural damage.

FLIGHT WITH EXTERNAL LOADS

48 For flights with external loads, refer to
the Load Factor Limits Table in Part 4, to
obtain G and speed limits and special manoeuvre restrictions. The following comments
refer to general aircraft handling with each
specific external load. With all external loads,
take-off distances will be greater and the
rate-of-climb and acceleration reduced due to
increased aircraft drag and weight. Refer to
Part 4, to determine performance effects.

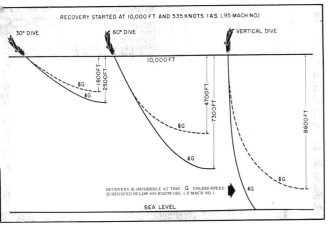

RECOVERY STARTED AT 10,000 FT AND 535 KNOTS IAS (.95 MACH NO.)

RECOVERY IS IMPOSSIBLE AT THIS G UNLESS SPEED
IS REDUCED BELOW 450 KNOTS IAS. (.8 MACH NO.)

Figure 2-5 Typical Dive Recovery

EMERGENCY HANDLING

EMERGENCY TAKE-OFF

GENERAL

1 The aircraft is ready for take-off as
soon as the engine is started. No warm-up
period is necessary.

EMERGENCY RELIGHTING IN FLIGHT

GENERAL

2 Relights may be attempted at altitudes
up to 35,000 feet. If malfunction of the normal
fuel system is suspected as the cause of engine
flameout, the relight should be made on the
emergency system and the engine should be
left on emergency system throughout the
remainder of the flight.

NORMAL SYSTEM RELIGHT

3 For normal system relights, turn off all
non-essential electrical equipment and proceed
as follows:

(a) Below 35,000 feet.

(1) If altitude permits, windmill engine
for one minute to evaporate excess fuel.

(2) With throttle OFF, place emergency
ignition switch ON.

(3) At 14% to 25% rpm, move and hold
throttle outboard for 4 to 6 seconds.

(4) Check that the low fuel pressure
warning light is out.

(5) Advance throttle slowly to idle stop.

(6) Allow rpm to stabilize before slowly
advancing throttle, to avoid possibility of
compressor stall.

(7) Place emergency ignition switch OFF.

EMERGENCY SYSTEM RELIGHT

4 For emergency system relights turn off
all non-essential electrical equipment and
proceed as follows:

(a) Move throttle to the OFF position.

(b) Place emergency ignition switch and
emergency fuel control switch on. This can be
done simultaneously. Low pressure fuel warning light should be out.

(c) At 14% to 25% rpm move and hold
throttle outboard for 4 to 6 seconds.

(d) Advance throttle slowly around the
horn to the idle stop if above 20,000 feet taking
4 to 6 seconds to complete the movement. If
below 20,000 feet advance throttle slowly
around the horn to approximately one half inch
forward of the idle stop, taking four to six
seconds to complete the movement.

(e) When relight has occurred as indicated
by a rise in exhaust temperature, advance the
throttle smoothly from the idle stop position.

NOTE

When operating with the emergency
system all accelerations are manually
controlled. Slow, steady movements of
the throttle must be made to prevent
over-temperature or possible compressor stall.

(f) Place emergency ignition switch OFF.

NOTE

Except at very low level where time is
critical, allow the engine to windmill at
14% to 20% rpm to clear it of unburned
fuel. A relight on emergency should not
be attempted at altitudes above 30,000
feet. At these altitudes it is preferable
to adjust the gliding speed to keep the
generator output, and depending on altitude 210 to 260 knots will be required to
maintain this rpm. However, above 20%
rpm a successful relight may not occur.

ENGINE FAILURE

ENGINE FAILURE DURING TAKE-OFF

5 Proceed as follows:

(a) Throttle control OFF.

(b) Apply brakes as necessary.

(c) Jettisoning of the canopy is a decision which must be made by the pilot according to the dictates of the situation. It is recommended that the canopy be jettisoned by use of the alternate release handle.

6 Decision on whether to retract LANDING GEAR or not must be left to the pilot taking into account availability of runway barrier, speed of aircraft and condition of overshoot area. If the decision is made to retract LANDING GEAR, proceed as follows:

(a) Press bomb-rocket-tank jettison button when bombs, rockets or drop tanks are installed.

NOTE

Rockets cannot be jettisoned electrically when weight of aircraft is on gear.

(b) Landing gear handle UP. Hold gear emergency up button depressed until gear retracts. On aircraft 23720 and subsequent, and on previous aircraft so modified, it is not necessary to hold the button depressed, as a retract relay, actuated by momentary depression of the up button, holds the UP selection.

(c) Engine master, generator and battery-switches OFF.

CAUTION

Leave the battery-starter switch until last so that power is still available to close the fuel shut-off valve when the engine master switch is turned OFF.

(d) Manually lock shoulder harness.

ENGINE FAILURE ON INITIAL CLIMB

7 If the engine fails on take-off after the aircraft is airborne, and if sufficient height can be obtained for a safe ejection, BAIL OUT. If not, prepare for an emergency landing. If sufficient runway is available to use the crash barrier it is recommended that the pilot leave the landing gear down. If the end of the runway has been passed, or no barrier is available it is recommended that the pilot leave the landing gear in the last position selected and concentrate on making a slow controlled landing with wings level and carry out those actions which will prevent fire.

(a) Throttle control OFF.

(b) Jettison external stores.

(c) Jettisoning of the canopy is a decision which must be made by the pilot according to the dictates of the situation. It is recommended that the canopy be jettisoned by use of the alternate release handle.

(d) Check flaps control lever DOWN.

(e) Engine master, generator and battery starter switches off before ground contact.

CAUTION

Leave the battery-starter switch until last so that power is still available to close the fuel shut-off valve when the engine master switch is turned OFF.

(f) Manually lock shoulder harness.

(g) Land straight ahead.

ENGINE FAILURE DURING FLIGHT

8 If engine failure occurs during flight, proceed as follows:

(a) Throttle control OFF.

(b) Establish glide at 185 knots IAS with gear and flaps up and speed brakes closed for maximum glide distance.

(c) Turn off non-essential electrical equipment.

(d) Attempt an air restart. (Refer to paras. 2, 3 and 4 preceding).

(e) If an air restart is impossible and a runway can be reached, prepare to carry out a forced landing. If drop tanks are empty, retain them, otherwise jettison all external load.

(f) If no runway is available, bail out. If a forced landing is contemplated, maintaining the glide at 185 knots IAS (gear and flaps up, speed brakes in), will provide the maximum gliding distance. Unless the engine is damaged, it will windmill at sufficient speed to provide power for the hydraulic system, although landing gear operation is slower than usual. Therefore, if an emergency wheels-down landing is contemplated, use the landing gear emergency release, allowing sufficient time for the operation. The flight control hydraulic system will operate normally. Excessive use of the controls should be avoided in order to conserve accumulator pressure. At normal gliding speeds, engine windmilling does not provide adequate generator output and the battery is then the only source of electrical power. With engine master switch, IFF radar, radio, armament equipment, pitot heater and lights turned off, the battery can supply power for approximately 5 to 10 minutes, provided that the alternate flight controls are not used.

WARNING

If engine damage prevents windmilling, causing normal hydraulic system pressure failure, the automatic operation of the alternate flight control hydraulic pump imposes the maximum drain on battery power and results in minimum duration of battery output. Should engine seizure occur and sufficient altitude remain to permit successful ejection, abandon the aircraft.

COMPRESSOR STALL AND RECOVERY

COMPRESSOR STALL

9 When the airflow through the compressor becomes less than required for a given rpm, the resultant relative airflow to the compressor blades is then above the angle of attack for stall and the individual blades stall in the same manner as a wing does. This is a compressor stall. Compressor stall can be initiated by rapid throttle movements during unstabilized compressor inlet conditions such as can occur during slipping or skidding manoeuvres or low airspeed, high angle of attack conditions particularly at high altitudes. If t movement is required during these cond a steady progressive motion of 3 to 4 s will produce the same rate of acceleratic less danger of initiating a stall.

10 The most common stall characte are simply a decrease in rpm to aroun 68% without noise or vibration and a temperature rise only.

(a) A change or surging in engine level, sometimes accompanied by loud re like pistol shots.

(b) An increase in aircraft vibration

(c) Extremely bad instances may vapour or smoke at the jet pipe and/or This may also be accompanied by a ra rising JPT.

RECOVERY

11 The following procedure has been d mined as both operationally affective technically sound and shall be used by all p in recovering from a recognized compre stall.

(a) Correct any abnormal attitude or ex loading.

(b) Immediately reduce throttle to idle

(c) Select AIR START switch ON.

(d) Move throttle gently onto the idle thus slowly reducing the fuel supply, unti stall clears. This will be evidenced cessation of rumble, slight increase in and a drop in JPT.

(e) Open throttle smoothly to desired p setting.

(f) Select AIR START switch ON.

NOTE

If the engine flames out during thi procedure or if recovery cannot b effected and pilot intentionally flame out the engine, relight is to be done o the normal fuel system.

NOTE

All compressor stalls are to be reported after landing. Record exhaust temperature and engine rpm at time of stall.

12 It is desirable, in view of the difficulty in distinguishing between true hang up and compressor stall, to treat both as compressor stall.

CAUTION

If possible try to reach a safe area, preferably a runway, before stop-cocking the engine in case a flame-out landing has to be made.

EMERGENCY FUEL SYSTEM OPERATION

GENERAL

13 The emergency fuel flow control system provides full manual control in case of failure of the normal fuel system. Its design is such that the fuel supply is constant at all altitudes for a fixed throttle setting. Thus, on a fixed throttle climb, the rpm will rise steadily with altitude, and throttle opening requirements for 100% rpm will decrease with altitude.

CAUTION

When the emergency fuel system is in operation, the engine fuel pumps are operating at maximum output and the Jet Pipe Temperature Limiter is inoperative therefore, indiscriminate use of the Emergency system must be avoided.

No changeover from the Emergency to Normal system shall be made other than in controlled test flights. When the changeover is required as in controlled test flights this shall be done at an altitude of 20,000 to 25,000 feet at an engine rpm of 85 to 95%.

(a) Retard throttle to IDLE.

(b) Place emergency fuel control switch ON.

(c) Advance throttle carefully.

(d) If a flameout results, attempt a restart if altitude permits.

WARNING

To prevent flameout with the emergency fuel system in operation, the throttle is to be manipulated carefully and in such a way that the engine speed is not allowed to drop below 40% until the engine is shut down.

JET PIPE TEMPERATURE LIMITER OVER-RIDE

14 The normal full throttle stop may be over-ridden by moving the throttle lever outboard and advancing it to the end of the quadrant. This action over-rides the JPT Limiter, at the same time breaking the wire tell-tale.

WARNING

This is a combat emergency device, the use of which may be accompanied by excessive jet pipe temperature, and is not to be used during normal flight operations. When used, the fact must be recorded in Form L14A.

TRIM FAILURE

HORIZONTAL TAIL NORMAL TRIM FAILURE

15 If a failure of the normal trim control for the horizontal tail occurs, the tail can be trimmed through use of the alternate longitudinal trim switch.

AILERON NORMAL TRIM FAILURE

16 If the normal aileron trim control fails, the aileron can be trimmed through use of the alternate lateral trim switch on the left console.

WING FLAP FAILURE

17 No emergency flap control system is provided. If unequal retraction or extension of the flaps occurs during normal flap operation, hold aircraft level and return flap control to original position. Land as soon as possible without attempting to operate the flaps. Aileron control is sufficient to overcome the rolling effect of unequal flap extension.

LANDING GEAR EMERGENCY OPERATION

LANDING GEAR FAILURE TO RETRACT

NOTE

If, when selecting landing gear UP the nose wheel fails to retract, or indicate UP, no reselection should be made until the position of the nose wheel can be ascertained. However, if the nose wheel retracts and the "D" door remains in the down position, reduce airspeed and re-cycle. If the nose wheel is down, or hanging in a partially retracted position, the landing gear should be selected DOWN, and a landing made when practicable. No further reselections should be made. If the nose wheel fails to indicate DOWN, do not reselect UP, but use emergency lowering procedure, and carry out procedure indicated in para. 17.

18 If it is necessary to retract the gear while the aircraft is on the ground, move the normal gear control handle to UP and hold emergency up button depressed until gear retracts. On aircraft 23720 and subsequent, and on previous aircraft so modified, it is not necessary to hold the button depressed as a retract relay actuated by momentary depression of the up button holds the UP selection.

LANDING GEAR EMERGENCY EXTENSION

19 When the landing gear indicators or the horn indicate one or more of the wheels are not locked down, see Figure 3-1, a visual check should be made by the control tower, if feasible. In the wheels down cycle, the downlock microswitches will not close the landing gear doors until all three wheels are down and locked. If the tower confirms that the wheels are down and the doors closed, the landing gear must be locked down, and continued evidence by the indicators or horn of an unsafe gear can be attributed to an electrical fault in the system.

CAUTION

If the utility system has failed and the emergency system has been used, the hydraulic nose wheel steering will be inoperative and much more than norma pressure will have to be applied to the brake pedals.

MALFUNCTION OF LANDING GEAR SELECTOR CONTROLS

20 Upon release of the emergency har following emergency extension of the land gear, malfunction of the landing gear cont

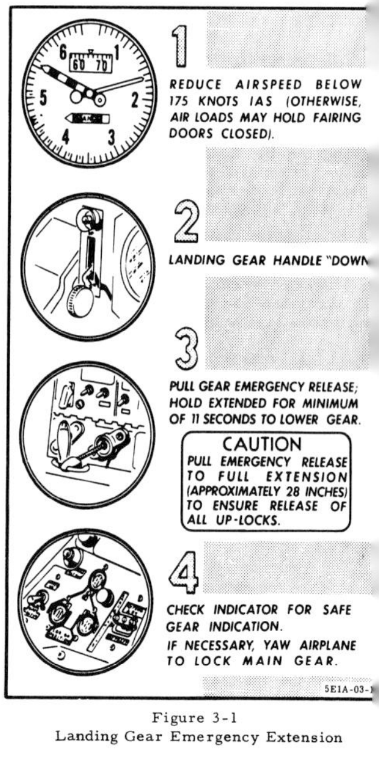

1
REDUCE AIRSPEED BELOW 175 KNOTS IAS (OTHERWISE, AIR LOADS MAY HOLD FAIRING DOORS CLOSED).
2
LANDING GEAR HANDLE "DOWN
3
PULL GEAR EMERGENCY RELEASE; HOLD EXTENDED FOR MINIMUM OF 11 SECONDS TO LOWER GEAR.
CAUTION
PULL EMERGENCY RELEASE TO FULL EXTENSION (APPROXIMATELY 28 INCHES) TO ENSURE RELEASE OF ALL UP-LOCKS.
4
CHECK INDICATOR FOR SAFE GEAR INDICATION.
IF NECESSARY, YAW AIRPLANE TO LOCK MAIN GEAR.
5E1A-03-1

Figure 3-1
Landing Gear Emergency Extension

.e or associated electrical components result in the main gear retracting again. s occurs, the landing gear control circuit-ker (fourth from rear, bottom row, left l) should be pulled out before further ation of the emergency release.

NOTE

the event of the landing gear control andle becoming jammed in the UP osition, the landing gear control circuit-reaker must be pulled out before perating the landing gear emergency xtension.

N GEAR DOWN, NOSE GEAR UP OR .OCKED

If the nose gear will not extend or lock 1 and if time and conditions permit, fire all nunition and expend any excess fuel to blish an aft centre of gravity and to mini-e fire hazard. If drop tanks are empty and ing can be made on a hard, prepared ace, retain drop tanks. Otherwise jettison external load. The landing should be made he following manner:

Jettisoning of the canopy is a decision ch must be made by the pilot according to lictates of the situation. It is recommended the canopy be jettisoned by use of the rnate release handle.

Plan approach to touchdown as near of runway as possible.

Make a normal approach with flaps and ed brakes open.

Throttle control OFF.

Just before touchdown, place engine ster, generator and battery-starter switches F.

CAUTION

Leave the battery-starter switch until last so that power is still available to close the fuel shut-off valve when the engine master switch is turned off.

Manually lock the shoulder harness.

(g) After touchdown, keep nose of aircraft off the ground as long as possible.

(h) Do not use brakes unless necessary.

NOTE

If nose gear is down but not locked, attempt to snap it into the locked position by making a touch-and-go landing. Make a power approach and touch the main gear to the runway with a slight bounce, then go around.

ONE MAIN GEAR UP OR UNLOCKED

22 If one or both main gears will not extend or lock down, jettison all external load and, if conditions permit, fire all ammunition and expend any excess fuel to minimize fire hazard. Retract gear and make a belly landing. If gear cannot be retracted, land on the runway with as many wheels down as possible. Use the following procedure:

(a) Jettisoning of the canopy is a decision which must be made by the pilot according to the dictates of the situation. It is recommended that the canopy be jettisoned by use of the alternate release handle.

(b) Just before touchdown, place throttle control, engine master, generator and battery-starter switches OFF.

CAUTION

Leave the battery-starter switch until last so that power is still available to close the fuel shut-off valve when the engine master switch is turned off.

(c) Manually lock shoulder harness.

COCKPIT PRESSURIZATION EMERGENCY OPERATION

EMERGENCY DEPRESSURIZATION

23 Should sudden depressurization of the cockpit be necessary, proceed as follows:

WARNING

Always have oxygen available for immediate use when flying above 10,000 feet with cockpit pressurized.

(a) Move cockpit pressure switch to RAM. Select oxygen regulator to 100%.

(b) If at high altitude, immediately descend to below 25,000 feet.

COOLING UNIT FAILURE

24 Failure of the cooling unit of the cockpit air conditioning and pressurizing system will allow air at high temperatures to enter the cockpit. If very high temperature air enters the cockpit, proceed as follows:

(a) If at high altitude, immediately descend to 20,000 feet or less.

(b) Move cockpit pressure switch to RAM.

OXYGEN SYSTEM EMERGENCY OPERATION

GENERAL

25 Should symptoms of anoxia occur or should the regulator become inoperative, immediately deflect the EMERGENCY toggle switch to the right or left and descend below 10,000 feet.

26 Whenever excessive carbon monoxide or noxious or irritating gases are present or suspected, the diluter lever should be set at 100% OXYGEN regardless of aircraft altitude until the danger is past.

ARMAMENT EMERGENCY OPERATION

BOMB, ROCKET AND CHEMICAL TANK EMERGENCY RELEASE

27 To jettison demolition bombs unarmed, press the bomb-rocket-tank jettison button. The bombs can also be dropped safe by having the bomb arming switch OFF, the demolition bomb single-all selector switch at ALL, the release selector switch at MANUAL RELEASE and then depressing the bomb-rocket release button on the stick grip.

28 Fragmentation bombs are automatically armed as they are released from the rack so that unarmed release of individual fragmentation bombs is impossible. However, if the complete fragmentation bomb rack is released with bombs installed, the bombs will be dropped safe. This unarmed release of fragmentation bombs is accomplished by depressing the bomb-rocket release button on the stick grip after positioning the fragmentation bomb selector switch at OFF, the demolition bomb single-all selector switch at ALL and the release selector switch at MANUAL RELEASE.

29 Rockets may be jettisoned by pressing the bomb-rocket-tank jettison button or by positioning the rocket fuse arming switch at DELAY or OFF and the rocket jettison switch at JETTISON READY, then depressing the bomb-rocket release button on the stick grip.

30 The chemical tanks or tow target canisters may be dropped by operation of the bomb-rocket-tank jettison button on the normal bomb release system.

ACTION IN EVENT OF FIRE

GENERAL

31 There is no fire extinguishing system in the aircraft. The fire warning system consists of two detector circuits, the forward circuit controlling a red cockpit warning light, marked FWD, and the aft circuit controlling an amber light, marked AFT. The forward circuit senses fire in the forward engine compartment; the aft circuit senses overheat or fire in the engine compartment aft of the firewall, (refer to Part 1, preceding). Since the aft compartment is much more resistant to immediate fire damage than the forward compartment, less drastic action is called for if the aft compartment fire warning light goes on.

FIRE DURING STARTING

32 If either fire warning light comes on during starting, or there is other indication of fire, proceed as follows:

(a) Throttle control OFF.

(b) Turn engine master and battery-starter switches OFF.

) Leave aircraft as quickly as possible.

RE DURING FLIGHT

If a fire warning light comes on immeately after becoming airborne or during ght, proceed as follows:

) If the FWD (Red) Warning Light comes in flight, immediate emergency action is andatory. The illumination of this warning ght may indicate an overheat condition but ould also be caused by a defective circuit. epending on the altitude, airspeed and flight onditions at the time, an attempt should be ade to determine whether the fire warning actual or false. The recommended proceure is as follows:

) Throttle control to IDLE.

2) Take immediate action to determine if fire exists by first ensuring that oxygen is n normal, next by either seeing or smelling moke or if in formation by having another ircraft check for fire. Check for abnormal nstrument indications, fuel, oil, hydraulic ressures. An overheat condition in the forward zone is not necessarily indicated on the P gauge.

3) If fire exists or smoke is detected ject immediately or force land if altitude does ot permit ejection.

4) If the warning light goes out when the hrottle is retarded and no other indications of ire exist, return to base or land at the nearest uitable aerodrome at a reduced power setting.

5) If the warning light remains on when he throttle is retarded stop cock the engine, engine master switch off. Regardless of whether the warning light remains on or goes out, eject or force land if altitude does not permit ejection, under no circumstances is he engine to be relit.

6) If at any time during the above procedures the pressure of fire is observed, the aircraft should be abandoned immediately.

b) If the AFT (amber) warning light comes on, adjust throttle to the minimum practical power to gain or maintain a safe ejection altitude. Check for abnormal jet pipe temperature or negative instrument readings due to burned electrical circuits, commence turn and check for trailing black smoke from the tail section. If no smoke is noted, maintain a safe ejection altitude at minimum practical power and return to the nearest base. Because of the possibility of fire reaching the aircraft controls, it is imperative to establish control effectiveness, before descending below safe ejection altitude, prior to landing. If at any time during flight the existence of fire becomes obvious abandon the aircraft.

SMOKE OR FUMES IN COCKPIT

34 If smoke or fumes should enter the cockpit, proceed as follows:

(a) Move cabin pressure control switch to RAM.

(b) Oxygen regulator diluter lever 100% OXYGEN.

(c) If not at too great a height, reduce airspeed to 215 knots IAS and open canopy.

ELECTRICAL FIRE

35 Circuit-breakers and fuses protect most of the electrical circuits and will tend to isolate an electrical fire. If an electrical fire occurs, turn battery and generator switches OFF and land as soon as possible, since the battery will last only from six to seven minutes if the flight control alternate hydraulic pump has to be used.

EXTERNAL LOAD EMERGENCY RELEASE

GENERAL

36 To drop any external load during an emergency in flight, proceed as follows:

(a) Push bomb-rocket-tank jettison button.

(b) Check to make sure load is released.

(c) If a check reveals that load did not release and if time permits, check circuit-breakers in and demolition bomb release selector switch at MANUAL RELEASE. Place demolition bomb single-all selector switch at ALL and rocket jettison switch at READY. Press bomb-rocket release button on stick grip.

ELECTRICAL SYSTEM EMERGENCY OPERATION

GENERAL

37 If a complete electrical failure should occur or if for any reason it becomes necessary to turn off both battery and generator, proceed as follows:

(a) If possible before turning off electrical power, reduce airspeed and adjust trim, as trim or flaps are not adjustable after switching off electrical power.

(b) The fuel booster pumps will be inoperative when electrical power is shut off. It may be necessary to reduce altitude and rpm in order to maintain satisfactory engine operation.

(c) Reduction of rpm for satisfactory engine operation without booster pumps may require that the aircraft be held in a slightly nose-high attitude to maintain altitude. If prolonged flight in this condition is necessary, approximately 21 Imperial gallons of fuel may be trapped in the aft fuselage tank since the transfer pump will also be inoperative. The actual quantity of fuel trapped will depend upon the total fuel in all tanks at the time of electrical failure. When sufficient altitude is available, some trapped fuel can be drained into the centre wing tank by levelling off or nosing down slightly for a short period.

(d) Land as soon as possible.

GENERATOR FAILURE

38 If the generator-off warning light illuminates, indicating generator failure or drop in generator output, all non-essential equipment should be turned off to reduce the load on the battery. If generator output falls off because of engine failure, the engine master switch should be moved to OFF to lessen battery loads. Battery output duration may be decreased by a number of variable factors including a low state of battery charge, excessive electrical loads and low battery temperature.

NOTE

If the generator fails, the IFF will be inoperative.

WARNING

In case the normal flight control hydraulic system fails while generator is out, battery power for alternate hydraulic pump operation will last only for a short and indeterminate time and the aircraft should be abandoned without delay.

GENERATOR OVERVOLTAGE

39 Generator overvoltage is indicated by the generator warning light illuminating. Attempt to bring the generator back into the circuit as follows:

(a) Momentarily hold generator switch at RESET, then turn switch ON. If the generator warning light goes out and the voltmeter reads normal system voltage, it indicates that the overvoltage was temporary.

(b) If the voltage cannot be brought within allowable limits, place generator switch OFF. Reduce the load on battery and land as soon as possible.

INVERTER FAILURE

40 Move instrument power switch to ALTERNATE when main instrument (three-phase) inverter off warning light is illuminated.

CAUTION

Loss of both three-phase inverters results in failure of the hydraulic and oil pressure gauges. These instruments, while operative, will provide erroneous indications as pointers may continue to register conditions which existed when the power failed.

FLIGHT CONTROL HYDRAULIC SYSTEM FAILURE

GENERAL

41 In case of failure in the normal flight control hydraulic system, the alternate system will automatically take over, as indicated by the alternate-on warning light. If the alternate system fails to take over automatically, move the flight control switch to ALTERNATE ON.

STEPS

1 Ensure instrument floodlights in stowed position, and, if at high altitude, pull ball handle on bailout bottle.

WARNING

LOWER HEAD AND BODY AS FAR AS POSSIBLE BEFORE JETTISONING CANOPY.

2 Lower head, pull up both hand grips to lock shoulder harness and jettison canopy.

NOTE

Should the canopy fail to jettison, open electrically at speeds below 215 knots IAS. Once open, airloads should remove the canopy when it is declutched. In the event of the canopy failing to open electrically it is possible to eject the seat through the canopy by pulling either trigger. It is important to first lower the seat fully, to permit the top of the seat rails to strike the canopy first and thereby shatter the plexiglas.

3 Rock the body back into the seat bringing the legs into the foot rests with the same motion.

4 Sit erect, ensure head hard back against headrest, chin tucked in, arms braced on arm rests.

5 Squeeze either seat ejection trigger.

6 After ejection and release of safety harness, kick away from seat.

NOTE

The present automatic parachute may be used successfully as low as 150 feet, in straight and level flight.

Figure 3-2 Ejection Seat Operation

WARNING

Because of the power output of the alternate pump, control movement should be held to a minimum to avoid the possibility of exhausting hydraulic accumulator pressure supply.

ABANDONING IN FLIGHT

GENERAL

42 All cases of emergency exit in flight should be made by means of the seat ejection. For seat ejection procedure, see Figure 3-2.

NOTE

The normal canopy jettison system is intended to be used only if followed by the emergency exit of the pilot. Once the canopy has been jettisoned by use of the right or left handgrips, the shoulder harness will be locked with no means for the pilot to release. Should it be necessary to jettison the canopy for any reason other than for emergency escape, the alternate canopy jettison release should be used.

EMERGENCY ENTRANCE

GENERAL

43 For emergency access to cockpit on the ground, if the canopy cannot be opened by the external electrical push-button, pull the emer-

gency canopy release on left of fuselage below the canopy frame and slide the ca to the rear of the fuselage deck.

CRASH LANDING

GENERAL

44 See Figure 3-3 for maximum glide tance with a dead engine. See Figure 3- procedure to follow in case of a forced lan

CAUTION

If utility hydraulic system is inoperative do not cycle the speed brakes at an time during the glide as remainin pressure will be exhausted and will n be available when needed for landing.

45 When practicing forced landing should be realised that a jet engine at id rpm continues to give several hundred po of thrust, whereas a powerless, windmil engine creates drag. If the speed brakes opened and the throttle set at 72%, the gli angle will approximate that given by a w milling engine with the undercarriage rai With the undercarriage lowered, set the thre at 69% rpm.

BELLY LANDING

46 If a belly landing is unavoidable, p ceed as follows:

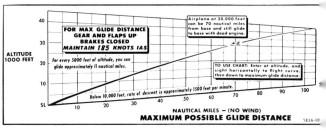

Figure 3-3 Glide Distance with Dead Engine

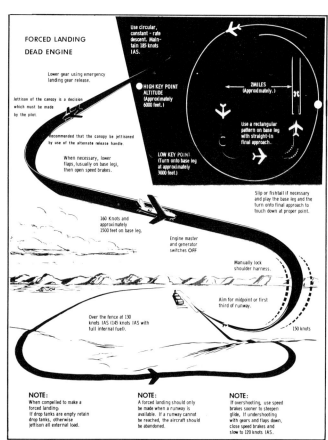

Figure 3-4 Forced Landing

(a) If drop tanks are empty and landing can be made on a hard, prepared surface, retain drop tanks. Otherwise, jettison all external stores.

(b) Jettisoning of the canopy is a decision which must be made by the pilot according to the dictates of the situation. It is recommended that the canopy be jettisoned by use of the alternate release handle.

(c) Establish glide at 185 knots.

(d) Make normal approach with flaps down, speed brakes open and undercarriage up.

(e) When sure of landing, throttle OFF.

(f) Just before touchdown, place engine master, generator and battery-starter switches OFF.

CAUTION

Leave the battery-starter switch until last so that power is still available to close the fuel shut-off valve when the engine master switch is turned off.

(g) Manually lock shoulder harness.

(h) Touchdown should be made in the normal landing attitude.

(j) Abandon the aircraft immediately forward motion stops.

DITCHING

GENERAL

47 Ditch only as a last resort. All emergency survival equipment is carried by the pilot and there is no advantage in riding the aircraft down. If altitude is not sufficient for emergency exit and ditching is unavoidable, proceed as follows:

NOTE

Inspect emergency equipment, parachute, life vest and raft pack before an overwater flight.

(a) Follow radio distress procedure.

(b) Jettison drop tanks, bombs, or rocket

(c) See that no personal equipment w foul when leaving the cockpit. Disconnect ant G suit and oxygen hose. Unlock parachu harness.

(d) Check gear up and speed brakes is

(e) Throttle control OFF.

(f) Jettison canopy by means of alternat canopy release.

(g) Lower wing flaps. Flaps collapse o impact and do not tend to make aircraft dive

(h) Place engine master, generator, an battery-starter switches OFF.

CAUTION

Leave the battery-starter switch until last so that power is still available to close the fuel shut-off valve when the engine master switch is turned off.

(j) Manually lock shoulder harness and tighten.

(k) Unless wind is high or sea is rough, plan approach parallel to any uniform swell pattern and try to touch down along wave crest just after crest passes. If wind is as high as 25 knots or surface is irregular, the best procedure is to approach into the wind and touch down on the falling side of a wave.

(m) Make normal approach and flare out to normal landing attitude, being careful to keep the nose high.

WARNING

Avoid ditching the aircraft in a near-level attitude, as a violent dive will result upon contact.